PENGUIN BOOKS

WELCOME TO KINGTON

Miles Kington was born in Northern Ireland in 1941, grew up in North Wales and was educated in the north of Scotland, which was all a big mistake as he was actually English. This meant he had lived the first twenty years of his life abroad *without ever leaving the country*. Finally, at the age when most people are leaving home, he came back to England at last only to find to his horror that everyone thought his name was Kingston. Hardly a day has gone by in his life without this exchange taking place . . .

'Name, please.'

'Kington.'

'Right, Mr Kingston . . .'

A plan for revenge was soon born. He would join the staff of *Punch* magazine and train as a humorous writer. He would leave *Punch* and become a columnist for *The Times*. He would leave *The Times* and become a columnist for the *Independent*. He would pay lots of money to Penguin Books to put out a collection of his *Independent* pieces with a photograph on the front of the sign greeting visitors to the handsome and correctly spelt town of Kington in Herefordshire. All this has now been done.

What remains to be seen is whether it gets people to spell his name properly.

If it doesn't, he has a contingency plan.

He will change his name by deed poll to Kingston.

MILES KINGTON

———

WELCOME TO KINGTON

PENGUIN BOOKS

PENGUIN BOOKS

Published by the Penguin Group
Penguin Books Ltd, 27 Wrights Lane, London W8 5TZ, England
Viking Penguin, a division of Penguin Books USA Inc.
375 Hudson Street, New York, New York 10014, USA
Penguin Books Australia Ltd, Ringwood, Victoria, Australia
Penguin Books Canada Ltd, 2801 John Street, Markham, Ontario, Canada L3R 1B4
Penguin Books (NZ) Ltd, 182–190 Wairau Road, Auckland 10, New Zealand

Penguin Books Ltd, Registered Offices: Harmondsworth, Middlesex, England

First published in Great Britain by Robson Books 1989
Published in Penguin Books 1990
1 3 5 7 9 10 8 6 4 2

Copyright © Miles Kington, 1989
All rights reserved

Printed in England by Clays Ltd, St Ives plc

Welcome to Kington

A Family Debt

MY father was a very advanced thinker in the field of educational theory. He had devised a system of student loans long before it was fashionable to talk about them. I found this out, suitably enough, the day before I was due to depart for university and leave my childhood behind me.

It hadn't been a bad childhood, all in all, and there were several moments I could look back on almost with affection. There was the time we had gone for donkey rides on a beach in North Wales, and my donkey had suddenly stampeded three miles down the sands. How we all laughed, except me. There was the time we had gone for a cycling holiday in Yorkshire and all our bicycles had been stolen, though I did not know this until my mother forced my father to give them back.

There were treats too, like the time when at 16 I was taken to a restaurant for the first time and given smoked salmon. 'This is one of the great dishes of the world, son,' my Dad told me. I thought it was awful: greasy, soapy and very thin. 'The boy's a fool,' said my father, lifting the salmon from my plate to his and tucking in before I could change my mind.

But all this seemed far behind as I filled in the labels for my university luggage and wrote out the placard saying 'OXFORD' with which I hoped to hitch-hike the next day. My parents had indeed given me the train fare, but, well trained by then, I had decided to save it.

'Might I have a word with you?' said my father, putting his head round the door.

'I don't have time for poker this evening, father,' I said. 'I am trying to get to university.'

'And before you go it would be as well to start with a clean sheet,' he said. 'I would appreciate prompt settlement of this.'

Whereupon he handed me a bill for £11,650. I looked at it, quite mystified.

'You have heard of student loans?' he asked.

'I don't think so.'

'It is a scheme under which students pay back the cost of their education afterwards.'

'But I have not been to university yet.'

'This is not for university. This is to cover the costs incurred while you grew up at home in the last 18 years.'

I was stunned. I knew my father had a keen business sense, but it had never occurred to me that I was a paying guest in my own home. Still, he had taught me two things about bills; always query them and never pay till you have no alternative.

'I take it you have an itemized account for the whole amount.'

'Of course.'

He handed over a a huge dossier. I ran my eye down it. I was being charged for nappies, baby clothes, toys, breakages, books, donkey rides in North Wales. . .

'Hold on,' I said. 'This can't be right. £3.50 for a donkey ride. They only cost 10p even today.'

'If you remember,' said my father, 'it was a very long donkey ride you took. You galloped off three miles down the coast and it was well into overtime before we recovered you. That ride cost your mother and me a lot of heartache and distress for which, I may say, we have not charged you, though we have added a small sum for wear and tear to the donkey.'

'You have charged for bicycles in Yorkshire,' I said. 'Those bicycles cost you nothing. Mother will vouch for that.'

'Foolish boy,' said my father, stung. 'Do you think that transfer of property from one person to another costs less simply because the first owner does not realize what is happening? A burglar has expenses like anyone else — which, I may say, he is not allowed to claim against tax.'

'Smoked salmon,' I said. 'I did not order the smoked salmon and I did not eat it. *You* ate it.'

There was a short silence.

'I am not an inflexible man. I will knock off the smoked salmon and send you a revised bill.'

To cut a long story short, we spent the next six months haggling over the bill and finally settled on a sum of £8,970, an amount which I managed to win comfortably at poker during my first term at Oxford. I took my parents out to dinner to celebrate.

'It wasn't really about the money,' said my father at the end of the meal, 'though that was nice. But in a very real sense you have now paid for your childhood and, unlike anyone else, will never again have feelings of debt or guilt towards your parents.'

'How true,' I said.

I paid the bill for dinner and entered the amount in a new account book freshly marked Parents' Declining Years.

'By the way,' I said, 'do you want this on account or do you wish to settle now?'

How To Be a Scrutable Oriental

WE ARE often told that our businessmen are slow to adapt to new trading conditions. A letter I have received this week paints a very different picture, and I am proud to print it in full.

Dear Mr Kington, As a businessman I am often told that, the Japanese being now the leading world power, we have to do business with them, and understand them, or perish. Fair enough; this makes sense. So I recently enrolled in a 10-day course on "Getting inside the Japanese Mind", and thought you might be interested in the diary I kept of my progress.

Day One. It is true. I had not realized before just how much we think of our little island off Europe as the centre of the world. It is just a habit. Our new habit, our teacher says, will be to regard a little island off Asia as the centre of the world. Look, China is just over there. America is just over there. Japan is convenient for everywhere. Except Europe, of course. If you really have to go to Europe.

Day Two. It is true. I had not realized before how strange the Australians look. Our teacher is right: what a gawky, bony, ungraceful lot they are. And how strange they should have their country right here in the Orient. I wonder why the Japanese did not settle Australia long before they got there. I wonder why the Japanese have not colonized countries in Europe . . .

Day Three. It is quite true. I had not thought about it before, but it does seem crazy to call Australia Down Under. Down Under from where? From Japan, it is just across the way. Down Under, for a Japanese, is South Africa.

Our teacher says the secret is to think of everywhere in terms of Japan, not England. England is out in the Far West, after all.

Day Four. It is so true. I had not realized before just what round eyes and long noses we British have. I am not surprised the Japanese have kept themselves so racially pure over the years. Today I had strange unaccountable stirrings of animosity against the Koreans. I told my teacher. He smiled and said: Good, good, but tell nobody.

Day Five. I think I am getting used to raw fish now.

Day Six. It is an awful thing to say, but I have started thinking of Europe as a far-off place — and I live here! My wife says that I am a different person since I began this course. Well, I find her views

4

much less interesting than I used to. A wife's job is to run a home and family, not to share a man's life.

Day Seven. It is true. The Second World War looks different when not seen through parochial British eyes. In fact, the Germans, Italians and Russians really had nothing to do with the war at all. The British were out there, all right, but were busy losing Burma, Singapore and Malaya. It's amazing we managed to keep hold of India.

Odd, too, that it's called the *Second* World War. The Japanese were not involved in the First World War, were they? I find it rather disrespectful to the Japanese to call it the Second World War.

Day Eight. How big my wife is. Big and pastry-coloured. Ugh. And why must she insist on ruining food by cooking it?

Day Nine. One of the businessmen on the course told me the Japs were clever at making things all right, but they couldn't use them. I smiled politely, which I now do automatically when I hear rudeness, and asked what he meant. Well, he said, where were the famous Japanese motor-bicyclists, racing drivers and TV stars? Everyone can name six Japanese cameras; who has ever heard of a Japanese photographer?

I asked my teacher about this. He smiled and said: We Japanese make and sell the motor-bicycles, the Americans and Europeans buy them and fall off them. Who are the clever ones? We had a good laugh. He took me out drinking later. My wife stayed up to complain. I must get a new wife.

Day Ten. This has been a completely successful course for me, as I now see many things from the Japanese point of view and understand them much better. What I cannot understand is why anyone should want to buy British goods, such as my own, when they could get a Japanese alternative. From this point of view the course has been a total disaster. I also hate Clive James for what he says about Japanese TV.

Still, let us never forget there is so much Japanese money in Britain that we more or less own the place anyway.

Sorry; not we. They.

I have begun to have very strong urges to invade China. Is this normal? My teacher says: Yes, about every 50 years. Will it be soon, I ask? Shh — all in good time, he says.

The writer of the letter is now undergoing a successful course to see things through British eyes. But it is, nevertheless, a salutary letter, I think.

When YOU Are the Weakest Link in the Chain

TODAY, a complete novella about moving house.

'I don't believe it! I simply don't believe it!' shouted David Bedfellow into his telephone.

The telephone was the only thing left in his house, apart from a kettle and a wireless tuned nearly to Radio 1. Everything else had just been loaded into a huge van called Your Move, I Think, which was about to drive to his new abode and disgorge the whole lot again. It had taken seven hours to load.

'You must be joking! It can't be true!' shouted David Bedfellow into the phone.

If you have recently moved house, you will probably guess what had happened. David's solicitor had just rung him up to inform him than completion, which was due today, had been held up because of a hiccup further down the chain.

David's solicitor was called Mr Rintoft, of the firm of Rintoft, Grass and Bloor, and the only reason he dealt with Rintoft rather than the other two was that the other two were dead. The way Rintoft reacted, David sometimes thought he was dead as well. 'The only reason I have you as my solicitor, you know, is that you have been the old familiar, family solicitor firm for years,' David once told him. 'I could easily go out and find someone newish.'

'All solicitors are old family solicitors to someone,' said Mr Rintoft. 'Your new and fresh man would be a veteran to someone else. Why, I would be fresh and new to someone!'

'I simply do not credit it!' shouted David down the phone.

'Do you want us to go ahead with the van?' asked the man from Your Move, I Think.

'Yes! No! Wait a moment!' said David, having what looked like a heart attack but was only a minor nervous breakdown. The van-driver, who moved houses every day, was used to such seizures and went off to make a cup of tea and listen nearly to Radio 1.

Finally, they came to a compromise arrangement. David would move out of his old house but not into the new one. He would leave all his stuff in the van, which he would rent until completion took place.

'I can't go on like this, Rintoft,' he told his solicitor three days later. 'All my clothes are in the van. I have to buy a new white shirt every time I go to work.'

6

'As a matter of curiosity, where do you sleep at night?'

'In the van, too. Luckily, the sofa was left right at the back. But I can't go on like this. What's the hold-up in the chain and when can I complete?'

Rintoft shrugged.

'Hard to say. There is someone several purchases along who is holding things up.'

'But who!?'

'Can't tell you. Their solicitor won't tell us.'

'But solicitors are meant to help you!'

'Oh come now, Mr Bedfellow, let's have no talk like that.' Rintoft looked quite shocked. 'Solicitors are here to protect themselves, not their customers.'

'Do you know what I would like to happen?' said David. 'I would like everyone in Britain to agree not to buy a house for a whole year. Everyone. Then it would bankrupt all the estate agents, all the solicitors and all the surveyors in the country!'

'That is the sort of line which, in a theatre, would get a sitting ovation,' said Rintoft drily. 'Here in a solicitor's office it gets only a thin smile and that's more than it deserves. However, I will see what I can do.'

When David had been living in the van for 10 days (long enough to get a traffic fine, a rates demand and enrolment in the local Neighbourhood Watch Scheme), Rintoft summoned him again.

'Quite unofficially, I have been chasing down the chain of purchase until I have come to the man who is causing the trouble. It's someone by the name of Bedfellow.'

'Same name as me,' said David. 'Unusual.'

'It's a David Bedfellow. He is the seller of 24, Thackeray Avenue.'

'Unusual address,' said David, feeling rather strange. 'Same as mine.'

'The chain goes right round from you and finishes up at you. You are eight house purchases from yourself in either direction. If you remember, you gave instructions that your completion should not be finalized unless EVERYTHING was satisfactory. You have been holding up your own purchase. You are, if you don't mind my saying so, a right twit.'

'Anything else?'

'Yes. The only reason I go on working for you is that you are an old, familiar family customer. The temptation is very strong to go out and find a new and fresh customer.'

Which wasn't, thought David, half a bad remark for a solicitor.

The Case of the Vanishing County

AUTUMN! Season of mists and motorway madness! With the arrival of autumn, a chain of bonfires is lit the length and breadth of Britain, signifying, not that the Spanish Armada has arrived, but that it is time to wreathe the nearest contraflow system in smoke again . . .

You see, *writes a doctor*, the circulation depends on a very fine network of what we doctors call secondary roads and main arteries leading to this contraflow system HERE. If the traffic keeps going, well and good. If not, we get a build-up which we doctors call . . . anybody? . . . that's right: Gants Hill. Now, this blockage called Gants Hill is sometimes unpleasant, often chronic and always fatal, so what we do is . . . anybody? . . . that's right, cut it out. We simply cut out Gants Hill . . .

It came as a great shock to the inhabitants of Gants Hill when they found out.

One moment they were a traffic black spot on the way to Essex, the next moment they were thundering up the M1 in a large skip on a lorry marked WASTE MATERIAL, on the way to who knew where? It was but the matter of a moment to form a Residents' Complaints and Whingeing Committee, Chairman Eric Groin. Mr Groin rose to address the meeting.

'Point number one,' he said. 'Some of us are sick and tired of being saddled with silly surnames like Groin by so-called humorists who have nothing better to do than think up silly names like Groin. I therefore move that my name be changed to Eric Chandelier.'

'I second that,' said Mrs Groin, delirious at the thought of having a sensible name at last, and being able to write letters to the local paper.

'Point number two,' said Eric Chandelier, né Groin. 'We of Gants Hill have been cut out of the national road network and put into a skip travelling up the M1. What does this mean?'

'It means we have to change our post code,' said a voice.

'Yes, but what else does it mean?' cried Eric Chandelier.

Reader, have you ever been in Eric Chandelier's position? In charge of a committee full of idiots who can't see things as clearly as you can? And do you feel the temptation to get up and shout at them as loud as you can, *writes a doctor*? Well, don't. This is called

8

the Boris Yeltsin syndrome and can lead to very unpleasant circumstances, including loss of job and loss of nice Moscow address. Now back to our story.

'Look!' cried someone.

They were coming up to a sign on the M1 which read: 'You are now crossing the North-South divide. Please adjust your house prices.'

'None of us wants to live in the North!' they all wailed. 'Do something, Mr Chandelier!'

As if in answer to his unspoken prayer, the lorry swung off the M1 and up the slip road to the Pork Scratchings Service Area. Eric jumped out and went to see the driver.

'I am Eric Chandelier,' he said, very pompously, 'duly elected chairman of the Gants Hill Residents' Complaints and Whingeing Committee. I demand to know where we are going.'

'We're going inside for a cup of tea,' said the driver and vanished. Eric got slowly back into the skip.

'Well, chairman?' they said.

'It appears that Essex is being relocated,' said Eric, saying the first thing that came into his head. Saying the first thing that comes into your head, *writes a doctor*, can actually do your brain a lot of good, especially if you've been thinking a lot of old thoughts. Try and think three new things a day and come and see me again in a month.

'Yes,' said Eric, warming to his fantasy. 'They've decided that Essex is too much of an eyesore to have all in one place, so they're splitting it up and sending bits all round Britain. We're being sent to Preston, to blend in with Lancashire.'

As he spoke, another lorry drew up beside them, with a skip marked PART OF BILLERICAY. The inhabitants cheered and waved at the Gants Hill mob, asking where they were being sent and claiming that they were on their way to Ludlow.

'My God,' whispered Eric to himself. 'It's true, then.'

Yes, reader, it's true. Essex really is being relocated. It's nothing to do with the county being an eyesore, Lord bless you, no. It's just that the Ordnance Survey need to sell more maps to make money, and if they didn't change the maps now and again, how would they ever sell new ones for more money? And if they didn't move Essex round a bit, what purpose would there be in printing new ones?

You see, it all makes sense when you think about it, *writes a doctor*. Next, please.

With the Greatest Disrespect

TODAY I am lucky to have the services of one of Britain's top lawyers, Anthony Grifter, to answer all your questions on the intricacies of the English law.

Q. I recently got involved in an amicable divorce from my wife. The agreement was that she should get half the settlement and I should get the other half.

However, there seems to have been some mix-up over papers, because when the dust settled it turned out that my wife was now remarried to my solicitor, and that they have both got all the money between them. What can I do about this?

Anthony Grifter writes: Under English law this is perfectly valid, I'm afraid, and there is absolutely nothing you can do about it. You could try writing to the Law Society.

Q. One of the windscreen washers on my car is badly adjusted and tends to shoot water into the air rather than on to the windscreen. Several months ago, while standing at traffic lights, I mistakenly sprayed a bystander. I was amazed, a few days later, to have a writ served on me claiming that the washing-up liquid in the water had blinded the victim, a solicitor, that my washer was an offensive weapon, that I was guilty of grievous bodily harm — in short, they were claiming damages of £1,500,000. They have since been awarded this in court. What can I do about it?

A. Under English law, I'm afraid this is perfectly valid and there is absolutely nothing you can do about it. You could always try writing to the car manufacturers and asking them where you can get the washer adjusted so that it does not happen again.

Q. I recently successfully sued a large company for shoddy workmanship, and I was awarded compensation of £23,450.50p. To my amazement, my solicitor's fees came to exactly £23,450.50p. I suggested to him that this was a coincidence. He said that there was no coincidence and that his fees always came to the exact amount of the compensation involved. What can I do about this?

A. This, under English law is quite valid, I'm afraid, and there is nothing you can do about it. You could try writing to the Law Society again, I suppose.

Q. I was recently playing in a cricket match against a legal side, and was called upon to umpire while I was waiting to bat. I gave a solicitor out when he was patently l.b.w. He has since sued me for wrongful dismissal, loss of earnings, defamation of character, slander and heaven knows what else, and when our action came to court he was awarded £49,000 damages. What can I do about this?

A. I'm afraid that under English law this is all completely valid and there is nothing you can do. You could always try writing to the MCC.

Q. I recently left a message on my answering machine to the effect that I was unable to come to the phone and that if the caller left his name and phone number, I would call him back. Well, I was called by a well-known firm of solicitors who were trying to drum up business through random phone calls, but of course I didn't bother to get back to them. They then sued me on the grounds that my recorded message was a legal contract to ring them back; by not doing so, I had broken it. They were awarded punitive damages. What can I do about this?

A. Under English law this is quite valid and an extremely clever idea, and I wish I had thought of it. I am afraid there is nothing you can do about it, except perhaps write to the Law Society.

Q. I was recently arrested in the small Devon village of Fastbuckleigh on a charge of spitting in the street. I admitted my error (I had a nasty taste in my mouth at the time) but claimed that it was not against the law. The police said that it was not against English Lbzaw, but that Fastbuckleigh was twinned with the French town of Pimpol and that it was illegal under French law. I was therefore being arrested out of solidarity with their French twin. What can I do about this?

A. I'm afraid that under EC law this is quite valid and there is nothing you can do about it. You could always try writing to the Société de Loi.

Q. I recently wrote to the Law Society and received a reply as follows: 'Dear Sir, We have examined the complaint against your solicitor and find there is absolutely no basis for it.' In fact, I had only written to ask for advice with conveyancing.

A. Under the Law Society this is quite valid and there is nothing you can do about it. I suggest you try writing to the Conveyancing Society, if there is one, which I doubt.

Do you have questions about your legal experiences? Just write to Anthony Grifter and see where it gets you.

A Moving Experience

IN THESE days of mass-produced junk mail, it's nice to be re-minded occasionally that the old-fashioned hand-crafting of letters is still kept alive. The other day, I received the following, which I can only call an example of genuine craftsman-made junk mail:

Dear Householder,

If you are moving house in the near future, all you have to do is get Power Packers to do the moving for you. Simply tell us where you are going to, and where you are coming from, and we will do the rest. Was it not St Augustine himself who said: 'If only we knew where we were going to and where we were coming from'? That shows just how little St Augustine knew about house-moving. When you're on the move, don't hire cowboys like St Augustine; hire cowboys like Power Packers.

What happens is this. On the day before you want to move, you just put everything in little boxes. Then on the day itself we come along and advise you to repack everything in tea-chests. But they are not just ordinary tea-chests; they are tea-chests specially designed so that when you get to your new house, they will not quite go through the door. Any door. But that is no problem for us. We just unpack everything into little boxes.

That is because we are proud of the traditional British way of moving house. To take another example, an hour after the first load has departed we come to collect some more stuff. You then say:

'But my partner at the other end has just phoned to say that your first load hasn't arrived yet.'

We then say:

'Blimey, we must have taken it to the wrong house, it was 13 Dean Road, wasn't it, oh, 13 Dean *Grove*!'

Then we all have a good laugh, a cup of tea and another bash.

That's the way it's always been done in Britain.

Many movers, you will find, break things during the move, but we never do this. We break them before we leave. We actually provide an expert consultancy service on what to break and what not to break because many people, we find, insist on taking things with them that are far too valuable and fragile to be gallivanting round the landscape. We generally advise people to break these

12

before they start. If they disagree, we go ahead and break them anyway.

Do you have bushes lining the path to your old house? You won't by the time we've finished. We find that bushes too close to human habitation are a safety hazard and we will remove these at no extra cost.

There will be three of us helping you with the move. There will be one who answers to Ken, one who answers to Ted and one who answers to nothing at all. He is rather disturbed, as his whole family died recently in rather mysterious circumstances. He has a special function — to take the blame for anything that goes wrong in such a way that you haven't the heart to blame him.

Before we arrive, have you remembered to cut off gas, electricity and water? You have? Then how on earth are we going to have cups of tea all day long? If it hadn't been for us, you wouldn't have thought of that, would you? Oh, and do remember to have radios in every room tuned to Radio 1, just off-station, with fading batteries. And if your house is more than 10 feet from the road, please make arrangements for a new access road to be built.

You can safely leave the rest to us, though you are very welcome to lend a hand if you want. Load the van, if you want. Drive it too, for all we care. That's our slogan at Power Packers: 'As if we cared'. Just one more thing. Have a large van standing by with three men in white coats. They may not be necessary to take you away at the end of the day, but who knows?

Oh, and pets. If you have cats or dogs, just tell us whether you want them to arrive a) alive, b) dead, c) somewhere in Yorkshire by mistake.

So, that's it. All you have to do is drop us a line saying the day you want to move out and naming another day if we can't make it that day. The rest is up to us. We also do funerals, by the way. Just pop the body in a tea-chest and we'll be around as soon as we can. We also have very competitive rates for the removal of small, unsightly rural bridges, the blocking of canals, major motorway pile-ups, demolition and conventional warfare.

Drop us a line and remember the name. Power Packers. 'See if we care.' Once you've moved with us, you'll never move again.

That Certain Smile

I WASN'T really going to write about my four-week-old son just yet. Not, I thought, until he was nearing 21 years old and able to fight back, but something has just happened which can't wait for 20 years and needs discussing right now. The health visitor has told his mother and me that within a week or so we can expect him to give us a 'social smile'.

This worries me a lot. I think I know what she means, mark you. She means that for the first few weeks a baby produces false smiles caused by wind, or rain, or plummeting shares, and that real, person-to-person smiles only come after that. That's what she means by 'a social smile'. But it still worries me.

I've been mixing with adults for more than 20 years, after all, and I have come to fear and distrust the social smile. There are so many kinds, especially at parties. There's the kind that says: 'I remember your name, but I bet you don't remember mine.' There's the kind that says: 'Excuse me, I want to squeeze past you, but I don't want to talk to you.'

Other messages conveyed by the social smile are:

'I have a much funnier story than yours, which I will tell as soon as you've finished.'

'I know the people you're talking about rather better than you do.'

'I am smiling and looking over your shoulder in case someone more interesting than you comes in the room.'

There are even people who go through the whole of life with a faint social smile playing round their lips, as if they are in line for a Sainthood. They worry me most, because nobody can have a reason to smile all the time. What I want to know is: when he produces his first social smile, which will it be?

At the moment, I am getting a great variety of expressions from him, all except the social smile. I am getting the social frown, the social yawn, the social burp, the social pursed lips and raising of the eyebrows, and the social stare into the distance which pretends I'm not even there. That's very disconcerting. I am holding him and he is staring past my eyeline at someone more interesting behind me. But there's no one behind me. That's very odd. It's even more disconcerting, of course, when he stares straight at me and through me. Only four weeks old, and he's cutting me dead already.

What I want is just a plain old smile. I have a fantasy daydream of meeting him at a party, where he flashes me a smile and we move into conversation together . . .

'Hello! We've met somewhere, haven't we?'

'That's right. I'm your father.'

'Right! I didn't recognize you. Normally, when you're leaning over me, you've got that great damned light behind you, and I can't see a thing, so I just stare into space.'

'I'm sorry, I hadn't realized. I thought you were cutting me dead.'

'Not at all! Good heavens, you're one of the very few people I know in this world. You and the one who thinks I look like you.'

'Your mother.'

'That's the one! Dreary old party this, isn't it? Do you know anyone here?'

'No, not really. Can I get you anything to drink, by the way?'

'Yes, please. Mother's milk would be fine.'

That would be nice, a straightforward social smile. But I suspect it won't be like that at all — I suspect that the very first time he gives me a social smile, as opposed to a wind-aided smile, it will be in code, like a real adult social smile . . .

'You think you change nappies as well as Mum does, but you don't . . .'

'If you say "Who's a lovely baby, then?" once more, I'll throw up . . .'

'Is that the only song you know?'

'You haven't really gone and bought those BP shares, have you?'

'As you've been reading so much about getting the parent-child bonding going, I suppose the least I can do is flash you a smile . . .'

Maybe I'm worrying about this unnecessarily. Maybe if I just keep handing the peanuts round, and filling his glass up again, and emptying the ashtrays, as it were, he'll give me a social smile of his own accord one day, with no strings attached. But it's a long time coming. I mean, it's melancholy to think that, at the age of four weeks, my son may have gone off me already. Never smiled at me in his entire life, when I come to think of it.

On the other hand, I think I may have solved the mystery of those people who go through life with a faint, saintly smile hovering on their beatific faces 24 hours a day.

They have got wind.

Uncle Geoff Gets His Comeuppance

Today, a modern nature story for boys and girls.

'What's that bird, Uncle Geoff?' said Tandy.

Uncle Geoff, who knew all about nature, was out for a stroll in the countryside with his nephew and niece, Macintosh and Tandy.

'It's a heron,' said Uncle Geoff. 'It lives by the river and eats fish.'

The children had been well taught by him that, in nature, everything eats everything else.

'Are those other birds trying to eat the heron?'

The heron was in trouble, indeed. Two seagulls were harrying it, like two fighter planes buzzing an unwanted airliner, and, as they watched, the heron was driven right out of sight.

'No, children. But you'll remember me telling you before that seagulls are leaving the sea and coming inland for food (*See 'Uncle Geoff Visits the Town Dump'*) so obviously the seagulls find themselves fighting other birds for territory. I'm afraid the poor old heron has just been chucked out.'

'Why do you say "poor old heron", Uncle Geoff?' said Tandy. 'You said there was no room for pity in nature.'

Little smarty-pants, thought Uncle Geoff, but what he said was: 'Quite right, dear. I take your point. Now let's go down to the canal and look at the wild flowers I was telling you about.'

They turned off the lane on to the tow-path, where the British Waterways Board had recently cleared the banks of vegetation. Uncle Geoff swore.

'But surely, Uncle Geoff,' said Macintosh, 'the BWB has as much right to manipulate nature as anyone else. You've always taught us that . . .'

'Yes, yes,' said Uncle Geoff. 'Now, can anyone tell me what those people are doing in that field? Remember what I've taught you about observation and deduction.' (*See 'Uncle Geoff Helps the Police with Their Enquiries'*)

Not far away, several men were running about, shouting and waving.

'From their clothes I'd say they were city people,' said Tandy.

'But the colours, the dark greens and browns, are obviously intended as camouflage,' said Macintosh.

'And yet despite the camouflage they are desperately trying to attract attention.'

'So they must be . . .' said Uncle Geoff.

'A Fringe group rehearsing for Edinburgh,' said Macintosh promptly.

'Human scarecrows on a YTS scheme,' said Tandy.

'No, children,' said Uncle Geoff, 'they are . . .'

'Saboteurs,' said Tandy. 'Grouse shoot sabs. Surely you knew we knew that?'

'Funny how saboteurs, who love the birds, jump up and down to frighten them away, but farmers, who loathe them, do exactly the same thing,' said Macintosh.

I never thought of that, thought Uncle Geoff. Just then he spotted something odd in the undergrowth. It was a pair of shoes sticking out. There were feet in the shoes. He went to have a closer look.

'Oh, my God,' said Uncle Geoff. 'I think he's dead.'

'Gosh, let's have a look,' said Tandy. 'Hmm. Young man, smart clothes. Bad blow on the head.'

'Look at his trousers,' said Macintosh. 'Those oily stains just above the turn-up, and the damage to the fabric. Could only be caused by one thing.'

'Chewed up by a bicycle chain,' said Tandy. 'Let's have a look around.'

Sure enough, they found his bike in the rough grass a few yards further on.

'He must have been attacked and left for dead,' said Uncle Geoff.

'I think not,' said Macintosh. 'My guess is that he's a yuppie recently moved into the area — who else would cycle along the canal in smart clothes? — and was coming this way in the dark this morning when he hit that overhanging branch there.'

The presence of a few hairs and a touch of blood on the branch seemed to back up the children's surmise, and a deep groan showed that the cyclist was coming back to life.

'Funny thing,' mused Tandy, 'but the way people move into the country round here and displace the old residents is just like the seagulls driving the heron out. Still, that's nature for you. Ruthless, but realistic.'

'Well, children,' said Uncle Geoff, 'I ought to be getting back home now, but shall we have another nature walk next Sunday?'

'I don't think so, thanks, Uncle Geoff,' said Macintosh.

'We'll probably be busy with our computer,' said Tandy.

Unlce Geoff suddenly realized it had finally happened to him as well. Nature had just given him the order of the boot. (*See 'Uncle Geoff Goes for a Walk by Himself.'*)

Apartheid: a Solution at Last

THIS morning, as I have nothing particularly urgent to do, I thought I would try to solve the South African situation. To begin with, let's sum up everything we know about South Africa:

* It's the most beautiful country in the world and the richest in Africa. What a pity about the troubles, eh?
* The whites are fanatical about sport; they could beat anyone in the world at cricket and rugby if anyone ever agreed to play them.
* The white minority speak a sort of pidgin Dutch with a harsh accent, which thank heavens the blacks seem to have avoided picking up.
* It's the only country in the world where the constitution is based on colour differences.

Now, where does that leave us? Well, it leaves us with several suggestive lines of argument. For a start, what about the sporting approach? The normal attitude is to refuse to play the South Africans at any sport they like playing, in order to discomfit them.

But what about turning that inside out and allowing the South Africans to play us *only at sports they are bad at*? For the sports-conscious South Africans to be constantly thrashed by the rest of the world at table tennis, darts, *boules*, skiing and figure skating might bring them to their senses faster than anyone realizes. Pride goeth before a fall, and hell hath no fury like a Boer beaten at cribbage.

Again, the South Africans have brought a lot of fury down on themselves by being so rich. If they had one of the poorest countries in the world, it's safe to say that nobody would take a blind bit of notice of their troubles. They would be a sort of Haiti or Burma, stuck out on the end of Africa and totally ignored. All the South Africans have to do is give all their money away or go bankrupt. It would also help if they lived in a less beautiful country.

Alternatively, or even additionally, the South Africans could switch to a nicer language, with a softer accent. French, perhaps. Or Irish.

Who could get angry with a very poor Irish-speaking community, living at the unfashionable end of Africa and playing badminton rather badly? Even if they did have a spotty human rights record?

Already, just by addressing ourselves to the basics, we have come up with a better solution than those managed by any eminent persons.

However, this solution is not complete. It does not address itself to the root cause of the trouble: the question of colour. Let us not beat about the bush here. Every government in Africa is more or less dictatorial, more or less tribal, more or less corrupt. What makes South Africa different is that it is the only country with a white government, the only country where whites are oppressing blacks. If Mr Mugabe and his party were white, and Mr Nkomo and his persecuted party black, Mr Mugabe would be the most hated man in Africa.

(That is why we get so upset about South Africa: what we are saying to Mr Botha, in effect is: 'Stop behaving like an African government! Behave like a white people!' Our attitude is every bit as racist as theirs. We are much harder on a white regime than a black regime. When whites oppress whites as the Afrikaners do the English whites, or when blacks oppress blacks, as Zulus do other tribes, we hardly get upset at all.)

The trouble with South Africa, in other words, is not that the oppressed tribes are black. It is that the tribe doing the oppressing is white.

The solution is blindingly obvious. All white South Africans should black up. Yes, adopt black make-up, burnt cork, long sessions on sun-beds, whatever it takes, but if the ruling white South African tribe became just another black African tribe, I guarantee you that the problem would fade into the background, just as all the other African problems have faded into the background.

Whether the Afrikaners would agree to do it is another matter, but I am only here to provide solutions, not implement them. All I can say is that if they agreed to become a remote, impoverished, Irish-speaking, black tribe with a reputation for losing every game of croquet they ever played, they would be left strictly alone.

A frivolous solution, perhaps. But we've tried all the serious ones, and where did they ever get us?

19

One Life Story, Hardly Used

MY *recent speculations about the art of biography have led to a rather startling letter from a reader, which persuades me that there is more to life than I had realized. Here it is, in full . . .*

Dear Mr Kingston, You won't know my name as I am a ghost writer. That is, I specialize in fleshing out biographical details for people who are famous, but who are not known for their skill in writing. The point is, I was approached five years ago by someone very famous in showbiz who was constantly being asked to contribute anecdotes to celebrity anthologies in aid of charity. You know the sort of thing: Celebrity Schooldays in aid of famine relief, My Most Memorable Embarrassment for underprivileged children, My First Kiss for a hospital threatened with closure, and so on. I am sure you have received similar requests yourself.

(Yes, yes, thousands, and I fully intend to answer them as soon as I have the time. Just get on with the letter.)

The thing is, this particular personality had run out of interesting things which had happened to him, and he had just been asked to contribute a telling anecdote to a new charity collection of tales about travel hassles. He had used up both the travel hassles which had happened to him. Rather than let them down, he wanted me to write an ignominious travel anecdote for him.

Well, this was meat and drink to me, so I wrote a neatly turned version of an absolutely appalling yet hilarious episode which I had once suffered at Heathrow Airport, though to protect the guilty I changed the venue to Gatwick. This seemed to go down very well, so on subsequent occasions I furnished him with various demeaning episodes in my life, all of which I retold so as to make it seem as if they had happened to him.

What I didn't realize is that this celebrity does quite a lot of after-dinner speaking, event-opening, that sort of thing, and has begun over the last few years to use the anecdotes I have written for him. Apparently, they go down much better than the ones he wrote for himself. I didn't realize this was happening until I saw him one day on *Wogan* chatting to whoever runs the *Wogan* show when Sue Lawley can't make it.

'You once had a strange encounter with David Niven and a bar of soap, I believe,' said the host. 'Oh, yes, that was hilarious,' said my celebrity, and proceeded to tell at some length a story which had happened to *me*, which he had obviously picked up from one of the charity anecdotes I had written for him. (Actually, it wasn't David Niven, it was David Frost, and it wasn't a bar of soap, it was a banana.) The terrible thing was that he had obviously told the story enough times for it to be very convincing by now — even I was half taken in by it.

I should have called the whole thing off then, but the money was good and the work was effortless, so I carried on writing droll incidents for him, all based on my own misspent life. What I didn't realize was that meanwhile a publisher had approached him with an offer to print his life story — they obviously thought, on the basis of what he already had in print and his chat show material, that they could make another David Niven out of him.

You can probably guess what happened next. The celebrity came to me and asked me to ghost-write his life story, using all the material I'd written already and more like it.

'It's all very well doing that stuff for charity and even chat shows,' I said, 'but you can't put total fiction into your autobiography.'

'What do you mean, total fiction?' he said.

'Well, like the story about you and David Niven and the bar of soap.'

'But that really happened. I was there. It's in print. I can prove it.'

He wasn't joking. He really thought it had happened to him by now. I suddenly realized that he had told all these stories so often, and so well, that they had taken him over.

The upshot is that now I am ghost-writing an autobiography for a celebrity whose life has been so dull that almost everything in the book did not happen to him. Moreover, all those incidents did actually happen to someone else — me.

And I am now told by a solicitor that the events in my life which I have written up for him — and which he has paid for — may now legally belong to him! It strikes me that I am literally giving up my life for someone else.

What do you think? yours, etc.

Me? Personally, I think the letter is a total leg-pull, and if I had read it to the end before printing it, I certainly would not have used it. What do readers think?

Please Dispose of
This Article Carefully

ONE OF the biggest tragedies the brewing industry has to face is that there is only a limited number of words meaning barrel, and most of them have been used up already.

They are nice emotive words, like keg, vat, cask, butt and tun. They've got an honest, Anglo-Saxon, woody flavour about them. No mucking about, you might think, with a vat or a tun, no funny business with kegs or casks. You can always use them to sell beer.

Unfortunately, the funny business has already taken place. The earthy overtones of 'barrel' were somewhat tainted when Watneys decided to market Red Barrel, and suddenly the word reminded people of great chunks of red plastic full of fizzy beer made by chemists in white coats.

The word 'keg' became even more tainted when it was applied to the whole range of new fizzy beers which were not even contained in kegs, but in big tanker lorries and huge tanks. 'Tank beer', however, would not have had quite the right ring.

The word 'keg' might never have been discredited if it had not been for the rise of CAMRA, the Campaign for Real Ale, which sought to stem the flood of synthetic, unreal beer and demand the return of old-fashioned, fallible but tasty beer.

CAMRA cleverly used the words 'real' and 'ale' as rallying points. It cleverly got 'keg' stereotyped as a bad word. It got the words 'cask' and 'conditioned' and 'from the wood' accepted as good words, and it even got the brewers to brew old-fashioned real ale, and put it back in the pubs.

So there was a happy ending to the story, was there, daddy? Well, not quite, my child. What happened then was that people got a bit bored with beer all round and went over to drinking lager. Not real lager, either, but the equivalent of keg lager. They gave it nice-sounding German names, which they wrote out in hand-wrought Teutonic writing, to make it sound genuine, but most of it was not the sort of stuff a self-respecting German would drink. Still, in 20 years lager went from having about 1 per cent of the market to having nearly 50 per cent. That's not bad for a foreign, not very real drink.

The thing is that the true British instinct is represented not by

CAMRA, but by keg. The British prefer keg things. Things that are easy, and prepacked, and convenient. Baked beans in a tin are keg beans. Sauce in a bottle is keg sauce. Salad cream in a jar, stuffing in a packet, tea in a bag — it's all keg food.

If you drive early in the morning through British towns you will see left outside restaurant doors here and there big transparent bags of pre-cut potatoes, which by evening will have become chips. Greasy, not very warm, not very crisp chips. Keg potatoes.

From time to time serious-minded bodies like CAMRA or Egon Ronay or the *Good Food Guide* grimly set about lifting British taste out of the keg era, and for a while it seems to have worked, but while everyone is congratulating themselves on the rescue attempt, British taste is slipping back, like a drunk with a bottle secreted under his hospital pillow.

It is well known, for instance, that at last our taste in Indian food has been improved. No longer do we automatically take the vindaloo and Madras curry (or what you might call keg Indian food). Madhur Jaffrey and all those regional or vegetarian restaurants have taught us to be more aware. But the real result of the revolution lies on supermarket shelves, where every kind of Indian meal can now be bought in a packet: new keg Indian food.

It is sometimes said that motorway service food has lifted itself out of the keg age. In my experience, this is not true. What looks interesting and different on the motorway hot-plate somehow changes itself on the journey between pay-desk and motorway table back into keg food — and in any case, people who really want keg cooking now have a vast range of Happy Chefs and Little Eaters to choose from.

Another name for keg cooking is catering. The British prefer catering to cooking. They actually prefer fish fingers to fish, tomato soup to real soup and English bread sausages to foreign meat sausages.

They prefer instant coffee to real coffee. Britain is the only country in the world where, if you ask for a coffee, you get white instant coffee.

Gentlemen, I give you the toast. Keg coffee.

A Fatherly Turn for the Verse

CHRISTMAS comes but once a year,
  And when it comes, it brings good beer.

That was the first rhyme my father ever taught me, and for a while I thought it was actually a Christmas carol. My father was a brewer by profession, though, so he was entitled so to sing. Every year, before Christmas had properly arrived, the brewery would produce little power-packed bottles of Royal Wrexham Ale with a purple label, and he would proudly bring back some of the first batch. It tasted like barley liqueur and was said to have the strength of seven men or half a bottle of whisky or something like that. I loved it as a child but I haven't dared drink it as a grown-up.

We grew up with beer in the house as if it were a normal part of life, not a forbidden substance. The same was true of verse. My father knew thousands of scraps of verse which he would produce without warning, so regularly that I find I myself come out with them without thinking. I certainly had no intention of starting this piece with a rhyme about beer. Or indeed, one about tomatoes.

> To market, to market went my brother Jim,
> Somebody threw a tomato at him.
> Tomatoes are soft, they come in the skin,
> But this one wasn't, it came in the tin.

The strange thing about this was that he had wodges of poetry on his shelf, and never referred to it once. First editions of Robert Graves, Rupert Brooke and A E Housman told me that there had once been a time when he had read and liked poetry. But the only book he ever urged me to read was Harry Graham's *Ruthless Rhymes for Heartless Homes*, and the only verse he ever quoted was stuff on that deathless level . . .

> The boy stood on the burning deck,
> His pockets full of bombs,
> When one went off, the lot went off,
> And left him in his coms.

Just sitting here, I find they come back to me without even trying. Challenge me to quote a line of Robert Graves, and I would be lost. Challenge me to remember a hymn, and all I can come up with is:

> There is a happy land, far, far, away,
> Where they have ham and eggs three times a day.
> Oh, how those boys do yell,
> When they hear the breakfast bell,

                Oh, how those eggs do smell,
                Three times a day!

That was one of the longest pieces he ever taught me — well, I say taught, but really I just heard them at such regular intervals that they became part of me. It's odd looking back how much of it seems to have been about eating or drinking.

                If you ever go to Dolgellau,
                Don't stay at the Raven Hotel,
                There's nothing to put in your bellau,
                And no one to answer the bell.

It's extraordinary. I haven't thought of these for years. I wonder if my father is writing this piece for me? If so, I had better include the piece he was proudest of, and the one which he thought boasted rather better rhyming than the regular poets ever came up with. It's important, by the way, that you should know that a cassowary is a big kind of bird like an ostrich, or so he always told me.

                If I were a cassowary,
                On the plains of Timbuctoo,
                Then I'd eat a missionary.
                Boots and hat and hymn book too.

Being a brewer, he did things at Christmas that nobody else did, like taking me and my brother on a tour of various pubs handing out mysterious gift-wrapped parcels and getting others in exchange — generally, I seem to remember, he would give away bottles and receive things with feathers on or salmon recently retrieved from the River Dee. There would be visits to the sample cellar, the sawdust shrine in the depths of the brewery where new brews were tapped and tried. Best of all, there would be the Boxing Day visit to the football match; Wrexham against the world, us in the only pub in Britain which is actually inside a League football stand, and maybe a wee dram of Scotch at half-time . . .

                It was Christmas Day in the mortuary,
                The coldest day of the year,
                And one of the corpses sat up and said:
                It's flaming cold in here!
                When in came the mortuary keeper,
                His face all aflame with beer,
                And took one look at him, and said:
                You can't do that there 'ere!

Unlike all his other poems, this one seemed to be part of a much larger work, and I often urged him to tell me the rest. One day, one day, he would say. He never did. But he left me a lot to be going on with.

A Big Hand for the Little Player

WHY ARE all bridge columns so high-powered and inaccessible to the amateur? Today, as an experiment, I am bringing you a low-level bridge column which reflects the way most of us play the game.

It is very rare indeed for one player in a bridge game to get all the cards of one suit. It is almost unheard of for two players in the same hand to get all their cards in one suit. But recently a game was played in which the impossible happened: two players got all the cards of one suit — and it was the same suit! Yes, North received all 13 spades in the deal and so did West. The game was at a private function in a small town near Bristol and the hands looked like this.

NORTH: spades A K Q J 10 9 8 7 6 5 4 3 2.

WEST: spades A K Q J 10 9 8 7 6 5 4 3 2.

EAST: hearts Q J xxxx; diamonds xxx; clubs J xxx.

SOUTH: hearts A K xxxxx; diamonds xxx; clubs A xx.

To an experienced low-level bridge player, it is quite obvious what has happened. It's getting late; two or three bottles of wine have been opened and emptied; and two packs of cards with identical patterns have got muddled up by somebody who has dealt out half of one pack and half of the other. But of course none of the players realize this until the cards are revealed during the play, so the bidding is unusually interesting. It isn't often that two players in a game both have a perfect hand and the same hand at that.

South opened one heart, quite conventionally. North, of course, intends to ignore hearts altogether. For one thing, he hasn't got any; for another, as soon as spades are safely trumps, he aims to put down his hand and claim all 13 tricks, then phone the *Guinness Book of Records*. So he is leaning forward eagerly to make seven spades his opening bid when, to his utter astonishment, West bids four spades.

This is, on the face of it, out of the question. North has all the spades. West cannot have any. Yet he is bidding four spades! Either he is drunk or . . . Ah! North suddenly recalls hearing about the odd, little used Wickerman Convention which allows you to bid the one suit you *haven't* got as long as the other three are very strong, or something like that. So North visualizes West's hand as:

WEST: hearts A K Q J; diamonds A K Q J; clubs A K Q J 10.

Not wanting to provoke a bid of seven no-trumps, which would sabotage his 13 spades, North casually bids five spades. This paralyses the other three. South and East think the other two have gone stark staring mad and open a bottle of mineral water. West cannot think why North, who has no spades, can bid spades unless . . . Ah! He suddenly has a dim memory of the Wickerman Convention, which he has read about. He visualizes North's hand like this: NORTH: hearts A K Q J; diamonds A K Q J; clubs A K Q J 10.

To cut a long story short, North goes to seven spades and West doubles. North lays down his hand and says: 'All mine, I think.' So does West. They then go for each other's throats and it is all East and South can do to drag them apart. A spirited end to a lively game, which I would like to see duplicated at tournament level to see how expert players would deal with it.

Incidentally, I have had an interesting letter from a reader who says: 'My partner and I have devised an illegal bidding system based entirely on noises, so that by coughing, clearing my throat, nose blowing, etc, I can tell him exactly what is in my hand, and vice versa. We thought it was foolproof but the other day in a big competition my partner got a bad cold with uncontrollable symptoms, and we lost every game!'

This week's problem. In a domestic game the players are using an old pack of cards which lacks the queen of spades and the three of clubs. They use the two jokers instead, one of which has 'Queen of Spades' written on it, the other 'Three of Clubs'.

Sitting at South you are dealt one of these jokers, but when you look at the message it now reads: 'Darling — I *must* see you alone tonight — Shirley.' Shirley is your wife, and she has just dealt. You have an uneasy feeling that the message is not for you — she has not called you Darling for years — but for one of the other two players, both men.

What is your best course of action? 1. To assume it is the queen of spades and try a cautious one no-trump; 2. Ask for a re-deal; 3. confront her with the evidence and ruin a perfectly good bridge game; 4. write unobtrusively on the joker 'This is madness, Shirley — we must stop now' and put it back into circulation.

Answer next time.

Join Now and Get a Freemason

IT IS the biggest secret society in Britain. Almost all army and police officers are members. Many politicians belong. No arts festival could ever get off the ground without it. And yet very little is known about the middle class, as this sinister league is called. Today we bring you the truth about the most mentioned and least known of all brotherhoods.

Q. What is the main purpose of being in the middle class?

A. To have a friend who is a solicitor, architect or doctor, whom you can ring up informally in the evenings with your problems.

Q. Does it cost much to join the middle class?

A. About £10,000 a year, plus school fees.

Q. What do you get for this?

A. A great deal of free information (most of it untrustworthy) about share rises, planning regulations, schools, and wonderful little shops that sell octopus and mussels.

Q. How do you join the middle class?

A. You don't. You find you have become part of it.

Q. How do you know when you have become part of it?

A. You find yourself uttering certain key phrases.

Q. Any examples?

A. Yes. 'We must have them back to dinner some time'; 'A spot of golf'; 'Something a little stronger, perhaps?'; 'Did we send them a card?'; 'I wonder if you'd mind awfully if . . .'

Q. If what?

A. Nothing. That's just one of the phrases that you use in the middle class. It's a ritual that if you go into a shop you never just ask for something, but always use a circumlocution such as: 'Do you think I could bother you for . . .?'; 'Could I have one of your excellent . . .?'; or 'Is there any chance that you could let me have . . .?'

Q. Why does the middle class talk like this?

A. Because the members do not know how silly it sounds.

Q. What beliefs does the middle class hold?

A. That the Dordogne is the finest part of France. That Tuscany is the finest part of Italy. That Radio 4 is the finest part of the BBC. That everything gets ruined eventually.

Q. By whom?

A. The working class.

Q. Is nothing ever ruined by the middle class?

28

A. Oh, yes. Fulham. Covent Garden. The Isle of Dogs. Any village within 100 miles of London . . .

Q. Does the middle class call this being ruined?

A. No. They call it 'coming up in the world'.

Q. Does the middle class have special names for members to use?

A. Yes. For example, Sophie, Camilla, Jasper, Sacha, Emma, Teresa, Harriet, Tarquin, Giles, Auberon, Evelyn . . .

Q. I really meant pet names, secret code names.

A. Well, the men call their wives 'my better half'; 'the old girl'; 'the old trout'; 'herself'; etc. Is that the thing?

Q. No.

A. That's another thing. If you were a member of the middle class, you would never have said 'No'. You would never said 'Not exactly' or 'It wasn't quite what I had in mind'. A member of the middle class is honour bound not to say 'No' or 'Yes'. He has to think of a way round it, such as 'I hardly think so'; 'It's not beyond the bounds of possibility'; 'Not in so many words' or 'Stranger things have been known to happen'.

Q. What rituals does the middle class have?

A. Dinner parties at which nothing can be discussed except mortgages, education and children.

Q. What do they eat at these dinners?

A. A brilliant idea from Josceline Dimbleby. That lovely dish we had in Portugal. A vegetarian recipe which is apparently very popular in India. A few left-overs. Pot luck.

Q. What music do they listen to in the middle class?

A. They collect records until they are 20, then never buy anything new. At the age of 40, they suddenly discover opera and forget all about music. Actually, it's quite common for the middle class to be more interested in the way music is reproduced than the notes themselves.

Q. Well, I have to say that they don't sound a very sinister lot to me.

A. Good Lord, no, they wouldn't hurt a fly. It's only when you're outside an organization that you think it is sinister. The middle class is absolutely harmless. They're dedicated to preserving standards, that's all.

Q. Is that a typical piece of middle-class fudged reasoning and self-delusion?

A. Beyond all question of doubt.

If you'd like to know more about joining the middle class, why not become a member of the National Trust and read the Daily Telegraph?

God and Mammon in Merger Talks

AS PANIC spreads through the civilized world and the City of London, it's time to hear a calming voice, so today I have asked financial expert Walter Schubanger to answer all your questions about stocks and shares and bankruptcy.

Q. I recently became one of the three million small shareholders who decided to put their money into small shares. I now find that the value of my shares has fallen so low that, were I to sell them, I would lose a lot of money.

I had no idea this would happen when I entered on the exciting, adventurous life of a shareholder. What should I do? *FB of Leeds.*

Walter Schubanger writes: Well, Mr FB, what has happened is that you have now passed through the exciting, adventurous stage and entered the rueful, older-but-wiser, sadder-but-poorer phase.

Life is not all sunshine and flowers, you know. We must take the rough with the smooth, the tears with the laughter. But have no fear; there is a purpose in all this, a greater design that we can only guess at. And now, let us sing Hymn No 137.

Q. That's all very well, but what should I do? *FB of Leeds.*

Walter Schubanger writes: Rush out and panic sell.

Q. I recently failed to become one of the three million small shareholders who were rushing into the stock market. No, I thought, it's a mug's game buying in a bull market. And I reckon I was right.

But now that share prices are tumbling I think I might have a flutter. Any tips? *HR of Bradford.*

Walter Schubanger writes: Yes. Rush over to Leeds and contact a Mr FB, who, I happen to know, will sell to you very cheap.

Q. As a newcomer to share buying, I'm mystified by the phrase '£50bn was wiped off the share index overnight'. Money doesn't just vanish like that. Where does the £50bn go? Where is it now? And can I have some? — *JSM of London W11.*

Walter Schubanger writes: Believe me, I'm as mystified as you are. But that's one of the beauties of the share market — it is a thing of mystery and wonder, an inexplicable force of nature.

As the volcano speweth out fire and as the wind goeth where it listeth, so do the prices of shares rise and fall, as the smoke from a fire. Now, let us pray.

Q. Another thing. When they talk about a wave of panic selling, I presume someone is buying all these shares that nobody seems to want. But who? And is what they are doing called panic buying? *JSM again*.

Walter Schubanger writes: Remember, the whole idea of share dealing is to buy low and sell high. The prices are low now, so now is the time to get out and buy. As many shares as you can! Go on! Don't hang around! Rush out and do it now!

Q. But what happens if prices go on sinking after you've bought? *JSM*.

Walter Schubanger writes: Hmm. I hadn't thought of that. Well you know, money isn't everything. A poor man can be as happy as a rich man. Happiness does not come from great material wealth — let us, rather, lay up a great store of riches in our hearts and souls and turn from the gold and diamonds of Babylon. For there is more to be gained from one good deed than from a king's treasure house.

Q. Here, you're a rum-sounding share adviser to me. What's all this biblical talk, then? What's it all got to do with economic advice, eh? *VB of Exeter*.

Walter Schubanger writes: You're absolutely right — well spotted! I am not in fact Walter Schubanger, the well-known economist, who is at present in custody helping the police with the Guinness affair. I am his spiritual mentor, the Rev Arnold Brawn, whom he has asked to stand in for him.

But do not mock the Church as an other-worldly and naïve institution. Bodies like the Church and the Vatican have more money than the rest of you to put together. The Church didn't get rich by panic selling and buying, you know.

Q. How did it get rich, then? *VB of Exeter*.

Rev Arnold Brawn writes: Never you mind.

Q. After the recent storms, it occurred to me that one could do worse than sink all one's money into tree nurseries, forestry plantations, etc. With the demand for new trees, one could make a bomb. What do you think? *TOE of South Wales*.

Rev AB writes: It sounds to me as if you have a shrewd eye to the main chance. How would you like to take over this advice column next week? And now, let us sing Hymn No 43, during the course of which there will be a collection taken for Shareholders in Distress.

A Man Is Known by the
Companies He Keeps

*TODAY, a children's story. But it's a children's story in line with
modern educational theory: that the main object of going to school
is learning to be an entrepreneur. It is this beautiful thought which
shines through the story of:*

Billy and the Bicycle Shop

Billy used to go to school on the bus. He would get on the bus with
his friends in the morning, and they would compare notes on the
things they had shop-lifted they day before, and then they would
go to school. And every day the bus would pass a bicycle shop in
the middle of the big town, on which there was a curious notice.

'Get off that bus. It will never be yours. Sixpence a day will buy
you a bicycle.'

'What does it mean?' he asked his friend Frank.

'It means you can buy a bike on the never-never, ride to school
and save the bus fare,' said Frank who knew all about hire purchase
and was to become a famous businessman and go down for insider
dealing.

It seemed a good idea to Billy. One Saturday morning he went
to the bike shop and queued for hours and hours, holding a damp
sixpence, behind bearded people comparing different cotter pins.
When the time arrived to go home for the midday meal, he had
not been served, so he left. He had just learnt Rule No. 1 of the
business world: *'You never get served in a bike shop. And if
you do, you wait so long you could have made more money doing
something else in the same time.'*

Not a very important rule, admittedly, but it's a start. Rule 2 is
more important. *'Never give up.'* So Billy went back the following
Saturday. Again he couldn't get served. That shows that he had
forgotten Rule 1, doesn't it? And that Rule No. 2 wasn't foolproof.
So now he had learnt business Rule No. 3: *'If you can't get anywhere, don't give up — move up!'* In others words, if you can't buy
a bike, buy your own bus.

'Dear Sir,' wrote Billy to the bus company. 'I wish to buy a bus
from you. Would sixpence a day be a requisite sum?'

'Dear Mr Billy,' wrote back the bus manager. 'We do not sell
buses on hire purchase. We do not sell buses to children. In any

case, it would cost you about £2,000 to buy a bus. Have you thought about getting a bike?'

(This, incidentally, brings us in fleeting contact with Rule No. 4: *'Yes, it's hard doing a foreign business deal, but it's not much easier dealing with your own countrymen.'*)

Billy showed this letter to his friend, Frank, who was impressed with Billy's idea of getting a bus but not with his way of going about it. He suggested to Billy that he would find it much easier to buy a bus if he were a rich foreign buyer importing British buses to his own country.

'Dear Sir,' wrote Billy on special paper, 'The Middle Eastern country of which I am proud to be the transport minister is in the process of renovating its bus fleet. We would be very interested in buying 200 of your excellent buses. First, though, we would like to borrow one to try it out.'

'Dear Billy,' wrote back the bus company manager, 'We always like to hear from you, and it was nice to get another letter. Perhaps you could come round and show us which bus you were interested in.'

Yes, the busman was quite taken with Billy's brand of North London cheek (Rule No. 5: *'Nothing like Tottenham Chutzpah'*). When he left school he was offered a job in the bus company. He took it, and did well. Soon he bought a couple of second-hand buses and started his own charter coach company. By and by, he had expanded so much that he bought up the company he had started with, and then he diversified into property development and local council corruption until he had become a knight, and given a lot of money to the Tories, though not in that order.

One day he remembered the old bicycle shop and decided on a whim to go back to the place which had given him his first business idea. He found the place, but not the shop. It had been pulled down and redeveloped by Maxima Properties, said the notice. It was one of his own companies. As Sir Billy stared up at the concrete block which had replaced the little old bike shop, he felt a choking feeling come over him.

'A small heart attack, I'm afraid,' said the doctor. 'That's partly, if not mostly, because you haven't had any exercise since you left school. I'm going to put you on a bicycle machine to start with.'

The bicycle machine certainly made a big difference to Sir Billy. He had a major heart attack on it and died. He had just learnt Rule No. 6: *'Get off that bicycle machine. It will kill you. Sixpence a day will buy you a bus ride.'*

If You Can't Stand the Kitchen . . .

EVERY DAY sees the publication of a new cookbook or part publication (second issue FREE with the first part!) telling us how to make classic dishes in the privacy of our own home. What these wonderful works never tell us, though, is how to carry on between the making of classic dishes. They don't cater, in other words, for the cooks who find, halfway through making a soufflé, that all their eggs have been rotten since last Tuesday.

All this is put right today with the publication of a new part work called The Wisdom of the Kitchen. *You will find it right here in this column, starting this very moment.*

The Wisdom of the Kitchen

Part One

1. Don't throw away your butter paper when you unwrap a new pack of butter. Put it in your fridge. When friends and visitors go into your fridge, they will say to themselves: 'Ah, this is the kind of person who saves butter paper. How prudent and wise.' You can throw away your butter paper as soon as you get a new piece; there is absolutely no need ever to use it.

2. When pouring milk into coffee or tea, remember to pour from as great a height as is practicable, as this does away with the need to stir. Milk added gently to coffee from a height of half an inch tends to muddy but not blend with the coffee, and you have to spend ages looking for a teaspoon.

3. Stirring need never be done with the 'right' implement. Inexperienced cooks often spend hours looking for a teaspoon with which to stir coffee when the handle of a knife or even your little finger would have done just as well.

4. When you are chopping onions or apples, and a small bit falls on the floor, there is a great temptation to pick it up. Resist it. The experienced cook knows that other bits of onion or apple are about to join it on the floor and that the only wise course of action is to leave everything on the floor until all chopping and cutting is over.

It can then be picked up off the floor and thrown away or, if there is enough of it, washed and put back into the classic dish you are creating.

5. A stale egg looks like a fresh egg. There are various rough and ready ways of finding out if it is fresh, such as seeing if it floats or breaking it open and smelling it, but the only one which is sure fire

is writing the date of purchase on the shell as you as buy it. The art of writing on an egg without poking a pen through the shell is soon acquired, as indeed is a felt tip pen.

The outside of an egg is such a useful writing surface that in my household we use it for making small shopping lists or leaving notes for each other. The other day I was looking for an egg on which I had jotted down an idea for a great novel, but somebody had used it. I have never had a novel scrambled before.

6. Mould is never as bad as it looks. The inside of a green loaf can often be quite toastable. Mould on the outside of cheddar or other hard cheeses should not be served to the average sensitive diner, but can easily be grated or melted along with the rest of the cheese, and gives a pleasant green tinge to the classic dish you have just created. If you are asked any questions about it, the answer is: 'Derbyshire Sage cheese, actually'.

7. It is no use trying to empty a sugar bag. You will always hear more sugar rattling around inside an empty sugar bag. Just throw it away.

8. The same is true of flour, except that you cannot hear it. Another thing true of flour is that you cannot carry a spoonful of flour any distance in a kitchen without some of it falling off in a fine white spray. Any good cook cannot cook for more than half an hour without building up on the floor a mixture of fine flour, crunchy sugar, bits of onion freshly chopped and fragments of garlic skin. There will be a recipe involving all these delicious ingredients printed in Part Three of *The Wisdom of the Kitchen*.

9. When you leave vegetables so long that little sprouts have started to grow out of the side or shoots come out of the top, the normal course of action is to cut them off and throw them away. What a waste. Why not cut them off, cook them and serve them separately as a mystery new veg?

10. The surest sign of a good cook is that he or she has very few cookbooks in the kitchen and that most of the existing ones have food stains on almost every page. Go and put food all over your cookbooks. Better still, throw all your cookbooks away immediately and cut out Part One of *The Wisdom of the Kitchen*; pin it on your kitchen wall and throw tomato paste at it.

The Passion, the Power and the Story

WHAT is *Airport Paperback*?

Airport Paperback is just about the hugest, most monstrous success in publishing history, that's all!

It's sexy. It's outrageous. Yet it's also moving and emotional. Its action sweeps continents and the ebb and flow of the generations, yet it also tells of the quiet moments of the heart and the tender love of a woman for the novel she is writing. It's . . . *Airport Paperback*.

Airport Paperback tells the story of Emily, who was married to a man she quite liked. Surely fate had destined her to do more in life than clean up after someone, put his underwear in a washing-machine and make his dentist's appointments? And so it was that in her kitchen, or at the controls of her lonely two-action vacuum cleaner (it blows, it sucks), Emily allowed herself to dream. Power, intrigue and passionate love, and the clash of mighty business empires . . . these were the dreams that Emily had.

And one day a voice said; 'Write down your dreams. Tell the story of your innermost desires, but make them happen to other people. Write down this story in an exercise book. Take six years over it, in your quiet moments, your rare time off, when everyone thinks you are at the controls of your two-action vacuum cleaner.' Three-action, more like, thought Emily: blow, suck and break down. 'Not a bad joke,' said the voice. 'Put it in your . . .'

Airport Paperback! The story of how one woman fought against her fate and rose from the humdrum ashes of her life to bring a blazing bestseller into the world! Yes, for six long years Emily toiled away at her epic story and then she met Eric the publisher. 'It's not bad,' said Eric. 'Not bad at all.'

Emily blushed slightly at the condescending tone of this patronizing but handsome publisher, who had taken her out to eat in a posh London restaurant with big prices and tiny portions.

'I like the idea of writing a novel about the battle to control the world's airport bookshops. The idea that the world might be changed by the people who ordain what people shall read on holiday. I like it. We'll have to change a few things, of course. More sex. A few more jokes, perhaps — I liked the one about the vacuum cleaner.

'And then your novel will arise from this old exercise book like Cinderella going to the ball — it will appear in three lurid colours,

36

with an embossed title, a caption reading 'The Great New Bestseller' and a tribute saying 'You must read this – Jack Higgins'.'

'Oh, really? Any other changes?' said Emily defiantly.

'Yes,' said Eric, leaning forward and very lightly touching her on the cheek. 'To you. We're going to take you out of those dowdy clothes, and give you a beautiful new face and a lovely new name and you're going to be a star, little Emily.'

That summer the publishing world could only talk of two things: the runaway, bush-fire success of Emily's novel, and the intense heat caused by her whirlwind romance with Eric the publisher, which withered two marriages as it crackled and burnt. Then she flew to Hollywood to discuss the screen transformation of the novel which one in every three airline passengers was reading, and met the man who was to break her heart.

'I'm Jack,' he said. 'I'm going to be producing your film.'

And giving you a child and leaving you cruelly, he might have added, if only he had known. Emily was to write many more runaway successes and make many more films, but she was never again to know a love like Jack's. She acquired glamour and money and power, yes, but after Jack she hid her softness and warmth behind a high security wall. Many men believed it was no longer there.

Only her child, Oscar, named after her first award, knew differently. (If a girl, she was to have been called Emmy. Their dog was called Pulitzer.) For Oscar received all the love which she could no longer . . . etc. etc. When he grew up, he was to take revenge on Jack, the man she had never told him was his . . . etc. etc. But before that could happen, Oscar fell in love with . . . etc. etc.

Yes, it's all in *Airport Paperback!* It's the sizzling novel which strips the veneer from the glamorous world of airport fiction and shows you the seething jungle beneath! But is *Airport Paperback* the name of the book which Emily wrote? Or is it the book which tells the story of the book that Emily wrote? Or is it just the name of the book which Emily dreamt about writing but never did because she is still leaning on her two-action vacuum cleaner and weaving her fantasies?

Read *Airport Paperback* and find out!

The AA Book of Motorway Folk Songs

IT IS a great fallacy that no more folk songs are being written these days. I myself spend a great deal of time on the motorways of Britain, collecting the ballads, folk songs and epic ditties that are still being handed on orally, all about our modern road system. Here, for instance, is a lament I recently heard in the Newport Pagnell service area.

> Oh listen, you motorway drivers, to me
> and next time you stop at the WC,
> Make sure that you don't leave the key in the car
> And when you come back, find your car is afar.
> I was only away for a minute or two,
> But when I got back from the motorway loo,
> The space where my second-hand Bentley had been
> Was filled by a cheap British Leyland machine.
> Oh, where is my Bentley, the love of my life!
> And where, come to think, is my good lady wife?
> She went off, they told me, a moment ago
> With your car and a sales rep whose first name was Joe
> So next time you stop on the M for a pee,
> Don't trust your companion alone with the key.
> Take all the keys with you before you begin,
> And if it's a Bentley, then lock your wife in!

A touching tale, even if it is unlikely to happen to most of us. But we can all learn, I think, from a little ballad I was told by a man I met near Exeter.

> 'Twas at the approach to the M that I spied her,
> A-holding a placard with letters so bold:
> 'Chemistry student, going to Sheffield,
> Very good talker, twenty years old.'
> She stood there so pretty, my heart gave a flutter,
> So I pulled to the side, and over she walked;
> She got into the car and she talked and she talked
> And she talked and she talked and she talked
> Till I stopped at an exit and said to her firmly:
> 'I haven't the faintest what you're on about,
> But I know that you give me a pain in the backside,
> And I opened the door and chucked the girl out.
> And now when I go up the M1 to Sheffield,
> I drive with my personal placard in view:

'Marketing manager, now pushing fifty,
Happily listening to Radio Two.'

But all the shorter poems pale into insignificance beside this longer folk classic. Its full version contains 140 verses.

When I was but a little lad,
I asked this question of my Dad:
Oh, Dad, one thing can you explain
— Why do we drive in the middle lane?
Would it be a great mistake
If we pulled out to overtake?
Or would it really be so bad
If we were in the slow lane, Dad?
My father said to me, I'm sorry,
But I *will* not imitate a lorry,
Nor will I drive like a railway train
— The place for us is the middle lane.
Oh, I'm a middle laner,
I love the middle lane,
I drive down it to Dover
And drive right back again.
You can flash your blooming head lights
And hoot till you go insane,
But you'll never get me moving
From out the middle lane.
And now that I'm a full-grown man
I think I understand God's plan;
That some are naturally fast or slow,
But most down the middle lane should go.
And even when no car's in sight,
And I could pull to left or right,
I hear the little voice of Fate:
You stay right in the middle, mate!
And now, when my son, whose name is Wayne,
Says it's boring in the middle lane,
And asks me to go up to eighty,
I turn to him and say, Look, matey,
You're a middle laner,
You were born to the middle lane,
And every time you doubt it,
Just sing the old refrain . . .

Soon I hope to bring you the ballad of Eddie, the sales rep who drove from Leeds to London on the hard shoulder.

From God to Moses, off the Record

IT NOW seems almost certain that the Ten Commandments do not, in fact, represent the true thoughts of God. The whole trouble lies in the fact that no written record exists of the informal briefing sessions between Moses and God, and that what we now know as the Ten Commandments are only based on the rough notes made by Moses at the time of his conversations on Mount Sinai.

In Moses' defence, this can be blamed on the peculiar, even unsatisfactory system whereby God never communicated direct with his chosen people but preferred to give the Israelite leaders on off-the-record briefing. What made it worse was that Moses or Aaron were limited in their taking of notes to engraving them on stone, which by today's standards is quite slow technology.

In any case, what seems to have happened is this: there was thunder and lightning on Mount Sinai, and a thick cloud together with the voice of the trumpet, which was God's usual way of hinting to Moses that he would like a discreet word with him. Moses duly appeared in the Lord's presence, and – so far as we can reconstruct the conversation – the following exchange took place.

'God, I believe you have some shifts in policy which you wish to announce.'

'Yes, Moses, I have a few impending legislative shifts which I want to test out on the chosen people.'

'You mean you want me to go back and give them the gist of your current thinking – unattributably, of course – so that you can watch and see how they react, while I get all the blame?'

'Yes, that sort of thing.'

'Right, ready when you are.'

'First of all, I have it in mind to impose certain measures on graven images – the molten calf industry is getting quite out of hand.'

'They won't like that.'

'I intend to float the idea of a six-day working week, with the seventh designated as some sort of holy day.'

'They'll like that.'

'I have some rather complicated recommendations concerning neighbours' oxen . . .'

'Hold on a moment. 'A – tax – on – graven – '

'There's no need to get it down word for word, Moses. Just the bare bones will do.'

That's where the trouble seems to have started. God's carefully obscure fiscal and penal notions were sharpened by Moses into a brief resumé and given the catchy title of the Ten Commandments. No wonder God sent out more thunders and clouds to summon Moses back to his presence.

'I can hardly begin to tell you how furious I am, Moses. I'm getting a lot of flak for this. I give you a perfectly good rundown of my new measures, and you come out with this . . . this farrago of half-baked ideas.'

'Well, Lord, I based it carefully on the notes I took at the time.'

'May I see your notes?'

'I'm afraid they've been lost.'

'*Lost?*'

'Well, I brake the tablets.'

'You *brake* the tablets?'

'Yes. I waxed wroth when I saw the molten calf and dropped them. That's not the point, anyway. The point is that your proposals are always so vague that in order to get your message across, I have to make it into some sort of story. They're not going to listen to old Moses coming back from Mount Sinai if he says: 'Look, I've got some possible shifts in God's thinking to tell you about.' That's not news. I have to hit them with the Ten Commandments!'

'So my carefully guarded statement on image-engraving becomes: 'Thou shalt not make any graven image?' And my gradual rethinking on burglary and theft becomes: 'Thou shalt not steal . . .?''

'In a word: yes. I know these people. They'll remember all 10 commandments. They wouldn't have remembered a single one of your 167 policy points.'

'Are you saying you know the Israelites better than I do?'

'Well, yes, frankly I am. I'm with them night and day. You're up here on Mount Sinai or off round the world, always at high-level meetings . . . Incidentally, you said you were getting a lot of flak. Who from? I thought *you* were at the top of the organization?'

'Never you mind about that. Well, it looks as if we'll have to stick with your blasted Ten Commandments. But I tell you one thing. When we meet again so that I can give you the Book of Leviticus, it will be an agreed text. No notes, no sensational headlines. All right?'

'Suits me fine. Saves me work just to print a hand-out. But *I* can tell *you* one thing. Leviticus will never be famous the way my Ten Commandments will be.'

What's It All About, Then?

MANY of the most famous questions in the world, like 'What is truth?' and 'How much it that doggy in the window?' are only famous because nobody has ever answered them. Well, let's see what happens if we DO answer them, because today we tackle some of the great unanswered conundrums of all time.

What is this life if, full of care, we have no time to stand and stare?

Life seems very confusing to most people because what happens here on Earth is in fact our dream time. The real part of our life happens millions of miles away on the planet Zeutron, and when we go to sleep on Zeutron, we come here to do our dreaming. So, after a particularly 'bad' day here on Earth, trying to make ends meet or understand the poll tax, we wake up on Zeutron saying: 'Phew – that was terrible! Thanks goodness it was only a dream!'

Our life on Zeutron is very pleasant, and we have lots of time to stand and stare without even being arrested for behaving suspiciously.

Come, let me know what it is that makes a Scotsman happy?

Dr Johnson would have known nowadays that a Scotsman is made happy by seeing England beaten at sport.

What do women want?

Freud's famous question. The answer is, seeing England beaten, though only if they are Scotswomen. More generally, what women want is more empty cardboard boxes at Sainsbury check-outs, a more pleasant method of giving birth, better excuses from husbands, wider recognition of women's superior driving ability, freedom from cheap sexist jokes, an evening out with Barry Norman, a different-shaped bosom, men who genuinely do get changed by women, better designed push-chairs, a chance to reshape their relationships with their mothers, etc. *(Full list on request.)*

On the planet Zeutron all these things are considered normal, and women want nothing. Nor do elderly Viennese psychologists ask stupid questions.

Watchman, what of the night?

I admit that, if we all go back to Zeutron at night, this poses several problems. One, notably, concerns Australia, which has its night during our day. Does this mean that we take it in turns with the Aussies to go to Zeutron and never bump into them there? Yes, it does, mercifully. But what about people who work during the night here and sleep by day, like watchmen? Well, they go to the planet Phlegmon during our day, to get away from the Aussies on Zeutron.

Oh say, can you see by the dawn's early light?

Yes, of course you can. And what you can see is mostly TV crews who have got up early to film the dawn. Because of the angle of the light, which creates shadows, back-lighting, hazy effects, sharp detail, etc, dawn photography is much more dramatic than anything else, except sunset photography. During the rest of the day cameramen tend to yawn and say: 'The light's too flat.' That is why documentaries have an extraordinary number of shots of suns rising and setting, a sight in which the rest of us are not interested.

Interestingly, because film crews have to get up early here, that means they have to go to bed early on Zeutron, where they are generally thought to be party-poopers.

Is this a dagger which I see before me, the handle towards my hand?

No, it's a Zeutron cocktail stick. Sometimes the transition between Earth and Zeutron is a little indistinct, and just for a moment we on Earth see things on Zeutron before they fade away again.

There is no violence on Zeutron and hence no daggers; the most competitive thing that ever happens there is one of the frequent cocktail mixing competitions.

Who wants to be a millionaire?

Everyone except Ben Elton. Ben Elton is already an extremely rich man on Zeutron, which is why he can afford to have such nice, egalitarian dreams here.

Which of you has done this?

Not me, I was on Zeutron at the time.

Won't you come home, Bill Bailey?

This is just one of a series of folk sayings based on mysterious disappearances, like 'Has anyone here seen Kelly?', 'Kilroy was here', 'Lover, where can you be?', 'One of our planes is missing' and 'Where have all the flowers gone?'. The answers, as you probably all realize by now, is: on the planet Zeutron.

Where hast tha been since I saw thee?

To Zeutron, for the holiday of a lifetime.

(This information service has been sponsored by the Planet Zeutron Tourist Board. Zeutron – a nice place to be.)

43

Parlez-vous Body Language?

BODY LANGUAGE is used to transmit a great deal of information from one person to another, yet its existence has not so far been recognized in a court of law. Now all that has changed. Legal history is being made in a libel case where the libel is said to have been transmitted by body language – not words. To give you some idea of the uncharted territory involved, here is an extract . . .

Counsel: Now, Mr Welkin, you were being interviewed on a TV show last July, is that correct?

Welkin: That is correct. It was Barry Spoon Chatting For Half An Hour About This And That.

Judge: Just a moment. What was the programme called?

Counsel: That is its name, your Honour. It's very popular to have casual names for programmes now, like *Clive Anderson Talks Back*.

Judge: I thought he was a barrister.

Counsel: He was, my Lord. Now he is making a living as Clive Anderson.

Judge: Good Lord. Whatever next. Carry on.

Welkin: Well, you've got to realize that Barry Spoon is one of the new-style chat hosts. In the old days guests were respected on talk shows. Now they're just slagged off. The host is trying to be clever, see, like Jonathan Ross.

Judge: Is he also a barrister?

Counsel: Not yet, my Lord. At the moment Jonathan Ross just runs a TV chat show.

Judge: I see. Carry on.

Welkin: And I was on the Barry Spoon show to publicize my new book, *Cue For Laughter*. But Barry just took the mickey out of me the whole time by yawning and reading a book when I was talking, and generally making a right Charlie out of me.

Counsel: And you felt so incensed that you decided to sue him for libel, even though no libellous words were involved?

Welkin: Yes. Well, no. What actually happened was that a solicitor who'd seen the show rang me up and said that if we sued for libel, we might be on to a nice little earner. But it comes to the same thing.

Counsel: I see. Tell me about your book, *Cue for Laughter*.

Welkin: It's full of the hilarious things that have happened to me in my amazing life, for instance, there was the time when Sean Connery and I were in a golf tournament . . .

Counsel: This is not a chat show, Mr Welkin. You are here to press a charge of libel, not publicize a book. *Cue for Laughter* is about your work as a comedian, is it?

Welkin: No. I am a snooker player.

Counsel: I'm sorry. It is hard to tell the difference these days.

Judge: One moment, please. Who is this Nice Little Erna? Does she also run a chat show?

Counsel: No, my Lord. It is a demotic phrase for something that brings in a lot of cash without too much effort.

Judge: Like running a TV chat show.

Counsel: Possibly, my Lord.

Judge: Do you happen to know if any judges have gone on to run TV talk shows?

Counsel: Not unless you count Judge Pickles. He runs lots of chat shows, but only, I believe, as a guest . . .

Judge: Could be a big hit. I see it now. Lots of famous guests, and a judge making a bit of an old-fashioned fool of himself, just like a real court.

Counsel: Yes, my Lord.

Judge: It's all a façade, of course, you know that? I put on this who-are-the-Beatles?-act to lull people's suspicions. I'm actually as sharp as a razor.

Counsel: As your Lordship pleases.

Judge: I'll give you an example. In the last five minutes, whenever I've been talking, you have been looking at your watch, wearing an exaggeratedly polite smile, drumming your fingers on your notes and staring ostentatiously round the room. Do you know what that is called?

Counsel: Body language?

Judge: Sheer bloody insolence. I've a good mind to sue you for libel. Actually, if this Welkin chap wins this case here and sets a precedent, I might well go ahead and do it.

Counsel: Yes, my Lord.

Judge: Good. Carry on.

Counsel: Now, Mr Welkin, you claim that Mr Spoon libelled you by using body language. How would you define body language?

Welkin: Well, for example, what the judge is doing now is body language.

Counsel: You mean, getting a large briefcase out from under his chair, rummaging around in it and finally fishing out a telephone and dialling?

Welkin: Yes. Basically, he's saying: stuff the lot of you – I've got something more important to do.

Judge: Hello, is that the BBC? Could I speak to the man who deals with new ideas for chat shows?

More from this case soon, probably on BBC2.

A Stiff in Time

SOMETHING *a little different today, as we bring you a complete science fiction police thriller* . . . The East Wessex police force had a dead man they couldn't identify. They had tried everything, including slipping it by dead of night over the border into West Wessex and leaving it there. Next day it was back, with a note from the West Wessex police pinned to it: 'Do your own dirty work, lads.'

'What do you reckon, Bob?' said Inspector Target. 'Slip it into South Wessex?'

'No,' said Sergeant Bob Tremlow reluctantly. 'He's getting a bit shopworn as it is. His tie got pretty crumpled in the last move.'

They looked admiringly at the hideous green, blue and orange fantasy round the late departed's neck. It could only be an old school tie.

'If I had been to a school with ties like that, I'd conceal the fact,' said Target. 'Still, I suppose we'd better run it through the file.'

It isn't commonly known that the police have a file on old school ties, also on regimental insignia, cricket club blazers, livery company markings or anything which might help identify dead people who insist on wearing such things.

'Fat lot of good,' said Bob Tremlow. 'Say we come up with his old school. What do we do then? Check all people who ever went there? Bring the oldest teachers in to look at him and say' "Do you remember teaching this corpse French?"'

'Have you got a better idea?'

They sent the tie away for questioning. Three days later the answer came back: This tie belongs to no known school. The tie had been cleaned and pressed. They went down to the morgue, put it back on the man and stared at him again.

'He's looking better,' said the sergeant. 'Shall we get the rest of his clothes cleaned?'

'Look,' said Target, 'maybe it belongs to an overseas school, or a school that no longer does ties. I've got a friend in the haberdashery business who might recognize it. I'll give him a ring.'

It was a shot in a million, but sometimes shots in a million come off. The friend looked up the tie in his archives and revealed that it belonged to the old boys of Nossex Grammar School.

'Nossex?', said Bob Tremlow. '*Nossex*?'

'You know, I presume, that Wessex is short for West Saxon?', said

Target. 'And Essex means East Saxon?'

'And Sussex means . . .' said Bob, to whom it had never occurred before.

'Precisely. Nossex is the missing kingdom of the North Saxons. My haberdashery friend also told me something else. Nossex Grammar School was closed down in 1923.'

They considered the implications of this. A Nossex Old Grammarian could not be any younger than 90. Their man was 35 at most. Why would a young chap go around claiming membership of a school which hadn't produced an old boy for 65 years?

'I'm going to get a check done on the rest of his clothes,' said Inspector Target, who rather fancied the idea of haberdashery archives by now. When the results came through, he wasn't so happy. The manufacturers of the clothes worn by the dead man had all ceased trading before 1937.

'What we've got here,' said the sergeant,' is a man who was too poor to buy new clothes.'

'These are very nice clothes. They cost a small fortune.'

'What we've got here . . .' tried Tremlow again.

'Is a man who died in the 1930s,' said Target.

It was the only theory that fitted the facts. This man had left Nossex in the 1920s and died in, say, 1938. He hadn't been found until 1989, and he was still in perfect condition.

'But *how*?' said Tremlow.

'This may sound crazy,' said Target, 'so don't tell anyone I said so. But what if a 1930s police force had found a better method of getting rid of corpses than just slipping them into West Wessex? What if they could slip them *through a time-warp into another decade*? Pop! The mystery corpse vanishes from 1938. Pop! It reappears in 1989.'

'You've been watching too much telly, old son,' said Bob. 'Give us a bit of evidence at least.'

There was a knock and a constable came in.

'Sorry to interrupt, sir, but we've got something pretty weird out here. They've found a body in the street, dressed in pre-war gear with a newspaper in his hand.'

'So?'

'Well, the main headline in the paper says: Chamberlain Flies to Munich.'

There was a long silence. Then Bob Tremlow said: 'That sounds like evidence to me.'

Deadlier Than the Kale

I HAVE received a complaint from a reader. Why, she wants to know, are papers at the weekend full of hints on vegetable buying? Why is there never anything exciting? So here is the answer to your prayers — a complete holiday thriller for vegetable-lovers!

James Firkin had always wanted to go on a theme holiday and when he saw the ad in the paper he knew it was finally the one for him: 'What to do with those Left-over Vegetables — a Weekend Course'.

Reader, do not mock the apparent banality of James Firkin's interests. If your allotment left you with large quantities of huge orphan cauliflowers every autumn, you too would welcome suggestions. Let us applaud, rather, his initiative.

James arrived at Brady Manor on the Friday evening and joined his fellow pupils for a drink before the opening talk. They all had double vodkas while he had a tomato juice. They all chatted about Pavarotti's essentially non-*lieder* approach to singing while he told them how he had taken the B45379 to get there instead of the busy A1(M).

Again, do not condemn his tedious talk too hastily. Those vodka-drinking poseurs would never get to meet Mr Pavarotti, while at least James had met and got to know the B45379. Let us applaud, rather, his honesty.

'Welcome to this weekend course,' said the speaker. 'My name is Ronald. Tonight I am going straight to the technical side of the problem, and I shall describe how a single blow to the windpipe can produce instant, undetectable death. I have here a model . . .'

After about five minutes James plucked up enough courage to express his puzzlement.

'What about the cauliflowers?' he asked.

Ronald took off the thick glasses he affected, and stared at James. 'What cauliflowers?'

'How do cauliflowers fit into all this?'

Ronald thought.

'Well, I suppose you could bash someone on the side of a head with a cauliflower, but it's really too soft . . .'

'I came here to learn about left-over vegetables, not killing people,' said James, gaining courage. Ronald put back his thick glasses and stared at the Brady Manor timetable.

'The vegetable husbandry course is next weekend,' he said. 'You've come a week early. This is the Secret Service refresher course on how to kill people quietly and undetectably.'

There was a silence. James realized that he had blundered into a course which wasn't going to be a lot of help to him on his allotment.

Having applauded him twice, we are now, I think, honour-bound to give him a boo. Still, two cheers to one boo isn't a bad average. There is also the thought that James had blundered into a course designed to eliminate undesirables. Like James. Perhaps two cheers, two boos, would be nearer it.

'Could one of you please close the . . .' Ronald was about to say, but James realized in a flash of adrenalin that he was sitting alone in the back row. In a flash he was out of the door and running.

There followed a hectic chase (this will come over better in the film version) which ended up with James motionless face-down in the spinach bed of Brady Manor's vegetable garden and the rest of the class nowhere to be seen.

James was just about to get painfully to his feet and make his get-away in the gathering gloom, when a voice chilled his blood. It was Ronald's, about two feet away.

'All right, Mr Firkin. The game is up. I am about to employ silent, undetectable method No.5 on you. Just stand still for five seconds. Say goodbye if you like.'

James's first thought was to say goodbye. His second thought was: that's funny — I'm not standing up, I'm lying flat out.

Cautiously he parted the spinach fronds and saw Ronald holding a gun and blinking through his deep glasses at a scarecrow. James knew he had about 10 seconds before Ronald discovered he was trying to kill a suit of clothes stuffed with straw.

He felt around cautiously with his right hand and to his utter relief found a large round object lying on the ground. He raised it above his head and . . .

Ronald would have been interested to know that a cauliflower *is* hard enough to cause instant and painless death.

Cauliflowers are plentiful in the shops this weekend. Also suitable for causing instant death are nice hard cabbages, though large parsnips are only suitable for a knock-out blow. Leeks are not nearly woody enough yet, and should be bought only for eating.

Destination Brainwash

THERE are highly skilled teams of negotiators ready to deal with hijackers anywhere in the world. There are, it now turns out, highly trained teams of hijackers ready to deal with highly trained teams of negotiators anywhere in the world.

But what about training for the poor passengers? Where are the highly skilled passengers who can handle the role of hostage anywhere in the world? And why aren't ordinary air passengers being groomed for the role?

The answer, according to Adrian Wardour-Street, is that they are. Adrian is PR man for British Air Crisis Handling. For 20 years, they have been advising the British Airports Authority on how to train passengers for a possible kidnap. And what they have all been doing is *training us without our knowing it*.

'From the moment you enter Heathrow or Gatwick, you're being put through a gruelling toughening-up schedule,' says Adrian. 'You queue for hours at the check-in. You walk for miles down anonymous corridors. You are made to get on to buses. You arrive in faceless rooms with no apparent exit. You sit for hours. You are told that rows one to 18 can go on board. The plane starts to fill up without you . . .

'Well, this is all psychological conditioning. We know that during a hijack, the passengers will be given illogical orders, put through meaningless ordeals, disoriented until they don't know where they are and made to lose all their identity. *This is exactly what happens to them at Heathrow or Gatwick*. If they should be hijacked, they will already be well prepared. Many hijacks are not nearly so bad as getting through Heathrow.'

Does this mean that airport procedure could be a lot nicer than it is?

'Good Lord, it would be totally different. Take one example. We could eliminate queueing. From the time you go through the terminal doors to the time you get on to the plane, you are put through a repetitive queueing programme: at the check-in, the boarding pass inspection, the customs, the security, the passport control, the duty-free check-out, the satellite bus. By the time you get on to the plane, you've queued a dozen times. Your spirit is being broken. And when on the plane, do you sit down? No, you queue to find your seat.

'Now, it's taken ingenuity to devise this. It doesn't happen naturally. We spent months planning it. Occasionally, even now, we think of new forms of queueing – gangway queueing has come in recently, for instance. There is no need for any of it, but if you're going to be ready for a hijack, we must put you through it.'

Why do people put up with it?

'Beats me. I can't understand why they don't riot and storm the VIP lounges. But the lesson is that passengers will put up with almost anything. Even duty-free shops. Why the public should happily buy moronically large bottles of alcohol, give someone a scandalous profit on them and then be forced to carry them off in the world's most hideous yellow carrier bags after going through that ridiculous boarding pass palaver, is quite beyond all of us. Maybe we have trained you better than we thought.'

The hostages released during almost all hijacks complain that they were made to lose all sense of time and place, which again is not unknown to someone passing through Heathrow.

'Have you noticed that we ask people to turn up hours early? And then keep them waiting endlessly? Have you noticed that we flash signs up on the departures board like, 'Boarding Now Gate 14'? And you rush along to Gate 14 and nobody is boarding at all – they're all sitting around waiting again? Have you noticed that when you taxi out to the runway, it doesn't mean you're going to take off? Dislocation of time is all very carefully worked out.'

What about dislocation of place?

'Airports are designed to be nowhere. Airports are the negation of place.'

Yes, but granted that all this can prepare the passenger for the gruelling nature of a long hijack, what can British Air Crisis Handling devise to prepare us for the sudden mindless violence of a hijacker?

'Well, for God's sake don't print this in your paper,' says Adrian, 'but we're doing this as well. Have you ever wondered why there are so many near misses these days? Why do you think there was that sensational near miss on the ground at Gatwick this week? It's all part of our campaign to toughen you lot up for the inevitable fanatical hijack. Or do I mean soften you up? Anyway, the effect's the same.'

It's nice to know that we are being so well looked after.

You and Your Postcard: the Facts

YOU go away on holiday. You send everyone a nice postcard the very day you arrive. You get back two weeks later, saying 'Did you get my card?' Everyone says, No. It then arrives *the next day*.

Even if you send several cards to the same person at intervals, *all the cards arrive by the same post* the day after you return. You wonder fleetingly where all those cards can have got to; then you get on with life and forget all about it.

Well, now I can reveal the answer. Last week I was lucky enough to visit the little-known counterpart of the wine lake and the beef mountain, the Postcard Pile.

In the great Central Card Clearing Hall of the EC, I talked to Jean-Fritz Poggi, the man who is responsible for making sure that no card gets home too early.

'Every postcard which passes through Europe comes here,' he told me during one of the mandatory tea-breaks. 'And then stays here for a week. It is a compulsory ageing process through which all cards must go. Eggs have to go through it. Wine too. There is nothing odd about this.'

'So all our cards are put on one side and abandoned for a week?'

'Abandoned? Absolutely not,' says Poggi, looking shocked. 'We read every one. Take this one for instance.'

He took a card from a tottering pile marked 'Cow Pictures From Switzerland', and read out: 'Hello, Mum. Hello Dad. God, this is a boring country. The telly's all in German. See you Wednesday week. PS, could you feed the cat?'

'What does that tell you?' I asked.

'It tells us he will be back on Wednesday week, so we know to keep the card till thursday week. Let's try another one.'

He knocked over a pile marked 'Silly Pictures Of People in Dutch Caps', and took the bottom one.

'Hello, Mum. Hello, Brian. Hello, Shirley. God, Holland is a boring country and the telly is all in Dutch,' he read, 'but at least the beer is good. Back tomorrow. Love, Trevor. PS, could you feed the hamster? To the cat, if possible?'

'So you know from that card that he will be back from tomorrow and you can send the card off now?' I suggested.

Poggi smiled.

'Not quite. Think about it. If Trevor were really going back tomorrow, would he be sending a card – or instructions on pet-feeding? I think not. He is being clever, this Trevor; he is really returning next week but he is trying to fool us into sending the card early. He has failed.'

And Mr Poggi tossed the card into a basket marked 'Christmas or after'. A whistle blew. Mr Poggi drained his cup.

'End of the tea-break?' I inquired.

He nodded, but did not move.

'And start of the wine-break,' he said, getting out a glass and a bottle. 'When you get all these different nationalities working at a Common Market centre, you have to respect all the customs: Tea-break, two-hour lunch, wine-break, siesta, *Kaffee und Klatsch – mon Dieu,* it is hard work keeping up. Let us try another postcard.'

He raided a pile entitled 'Aerial Views of Pimples In the Atlantic' and selected a view of a Canary island. 'Hello, Gran. Hello, Grandad,' he intoned. 'God, Madeira is a boring island. The telly is all in Portuguese, but I'll be back in a month or two when this job is over, love Brian. PS, could you remember to pop round and feed Mum and Dad? Ta.'

'Well, that tells us one of two things,' said Poggi. 'One, he thinks he is on Madeira but he is actually in the Canaries, so no wonder he is bored. Two, he will not be home until 1989 and therefore comes into a special category.'

He tossed the postcard into a hopper marked 'Keep Till 1990, Then Send To Kuwait'.

'So if I've got it right,' I said, 'our postcards all arrive late because you keep them back.'

'And because the address is written so badly,' said Poggi, taking another drink. 'But mostly because we are so drunk when we are sorting them.'

He waved an expansive wave. It knocked over a huge tower of postcards labelled 'Glittering Ski Slope in Sunset, Could Be Anywhere', which fell forward in a slow curve and engulfed him. A card fluttered down at my feet. I picked it up and read:

'Max – I've decided it's safest to send the drugs by postcard, OK? You'll find a small dot under each stamp. I'm sending off 30,000 cards, which should give us enough of the stuff to be back in business. Nobody ever reads the messages on these cards, so don't worry. PS, God, Bolivia is boring. And the telly's all in Spanish.'

I put the card in Jean-Fritz's outstretched toes and left.

DIY Fiction Readers Start Here

TODAY we have a novel set in the business world. Apart from being shorter than the average novel, it is unusual in that you are the hero, and are given multiple choices at every turn. Have fun!

Your name is Terry Holmes and you have been a fireproof door salesman for 15 years. You enjoyed selling fireproof doors for the first 10 years but recently you have started to think that there may be more to life than stopping hotels burning down. You have just written your letter of resignation when the boss sends for you. What do you think he is going to tell you?

1. That you are not fireproof and are going to be. Fired, that is.

2. That they have just discovered the doors you have been selling for 15 years do not in fact repel flames.

3. That he wishes to adopt you as his legal son and leave you the firm.

4. That you are to be sent to the Annual Fireproof Door Sales Convention, which is a notoriously drunken shindig.

Hastily concealing your letter of resignation, you go home to pack your bags for your visit to the convention. When you arrive there you are handed a lapel badge with strict instructions to wear it at all times, as only this will gain you access to all meetings, parties, bars, etc. It is only later that you notice that your lapel badge does not say Terry Holmes, but Jerry Houser. How do you react?

1. You get it changed.

2. You assume that it is a misprint and change the name with your pen, making a hash of it.

3. You assume that it is not a misprint but that some fellow called Jerry Houser is going round with a lapel badge marked Terry Holmes, and you decide to wait till you meet him.

4. You start running up an enormous bar bill in the name of Jerry Houser, confident in the knowledge that you will never have to pay it.

After two days of the conference, you have made a lot of friends, thanks to Jerry Houser's bar bill. You have had a lot of fun trying to set fire to hotel doors late at night with your new chums, to see if they are fireproof. You have learnt a lot, eg that hotels don't like having their doors set fire to. You have also become used to being called Jerry, and have almost forgotten you were ever Terry.

However, one night someone behind you at the bar says: 'Jerry

Houser?', and when you turn round to say: 'Yes,' a man yells: 'Then take that, you bastard!' and swings a punch at you. Who do you assume this is?

1. He is the man in charge of the lapel badge system, and he feels you have let him down.

2. He is a man whose wife was once seduced by someone called Jerry Houser.

3. He is a man who was recently sold 500 fireproof doors by a man called Jerry Houser, all which have burnt down.

4. He *is* Jerry Houser and he has just found out about his bar bill.

Before you have time to test your assumption, you find yourself sprawling on the floor, dazed. As you get up, you realize that your lapel badge has been knocked off, so you automatically start to put it back on. As you do so, you realize that it has writing on *both* sides. On one side it says Jerry Houser, as you know; on the other it says in bigger letters 'Terry Holmes'.

In a flash you realize what has happened. You put the badge on back to front to begin with. Jerry Houser is the name of the firm that makes lapel badges!

Then the man knocks you down again. What do you you do?

1. Say: 'No, I am Terry Holmes and I would like to buy you a drink.'

2. Bite his ankles.

3. Get out your cordless phone and ring your boss at home to read out your letter of resignation.

4. Wake up and find it was all a dream, and you are sitting in the first-class compartment of your last train home. Unfortunately, while you were asleep you passed your station and you are now in some dark and abandoned siding.

You open the nearest window in the train and find it is snowing. What do you do?

1. Make your way to the phone box in Coach H and phone home to say you haven't the faintest idea where you are.

2. Make your way to the engine and attempt to drive home.

3. Make your way to the buffet bar situated towards the front of the train and try to break in.

4. Realize that you still haven't found out who the bloke was who knocked you down, and go to sleep again to find out.

Safely asleep again, you find yourself in a different dream in which you and and the Queen are together a lift. She turns to you and says: 'Which floor?' Do you – I'm sorry. I've run out of space. You'll have to carry on by yourself. Have fun!

The Pedal Squad

THE FIRST day out on his new bike, PC Wainwright caught his trousers in the chain.

The second day out on his new bike, he bought a pair of bike clips to protect his trousers and got a corner of his police cape caught in the wheel.

The third day out, he left his cape off and got wet.

'I'm fed up with this bleeding bicycle,' he grumbled back at the station. 'London bobby back in the saddle, indeed. Why don't they put us on flaming horseback and have done with it?'

'I might remind you,' said the Sergeant, who was given to annoying phrases like that, 'that we have a lot of policemen on horseback and nobody laughs at them.'

'It's not being laughed at I mind. It's being overtaken by mothers with prams.'

'One thing you would do well to bear in mind,' said the Sergeant, another of his irritating phrases, 'is that at least you don't have a siren and a flashing blue light on your head.'

'Yes, Sarge.'

The fourth day out, it was sunny and he felt better.

The fifth day out, he had the extreme pleasure of overtaking a police squad car. The car was stuck in a traffic jam in Brentford and PC Wainwright simply pedalled up the inside, waved to the occupants and turned left into a nearby street.

'The bike's not so bad when you get the hang of it, Sarge. You cover a lot of ground and start getting some lovely thigh muscles.'

'Maybe you'll start arresting some people soon, too,' said the Sergeant, which was what he always said whether you had a bike or not. But PC Wainwright's chance came sooner than he thought. He stopped in Acacia Avenue to look at a flash racing bike that had been left unattended and unlocked, and was bending over it when the owner arrived.

'This yours, son? You're asking for it to be stolen.'

'Thanks for the advice.'

'You've also got a defective reflector and no light fixtures. I could charge you for that.'

'I've got a better idea. Why don't you just piss off?'

PC Wainwright went red. Then he went for his notebook. Then he went quiet, as the bike owner produced an ID card and whispered in

56

his ear: 'Plainclothes bike squad. We've got a drugs suspect under surveillance across the road. Now piss off.'

PC Wainwright pedalled thoughtfully off, wondering just how far this police bike revolution was going to go. He could see it made sense to have plainclothes bike police, if only because nobody would expect it, but what next? Bike escorts for the Queen? The Queen on a bike . . .?

His reverie was interrupted by a curious sight in the High Street. Outside the bank there were three racing bikes. Normally PC Wainwright would never have noticed such a thing, but when you're into bikes, you start noticing everything on two wheels. He stopped. He paused. He didn't want to annoy more plainclothes policemen again. And as he was pausing, three men wearing balaclavas ran out of the bank, jumped on the bikes and shot away. PC Wainwright shot off in hopeless pursuit.

'It stands to reason,' said the Sarge later. 'Give the police a weapon and the villains follow suit. When we got guns, they started going armed. Now we've got bikes, they're getting bikes. Ideal for getaways in heavy traffic. Now, give us that third bike's description again.'

'Red painted Claude Butler frame, blue tape on handlebars, NUCLEAR ENERGY? NO THANKS! sticker on frame . . .'

PC Wainwright's detailed description led to an arrest three days later, and even the Sergeant unbent enough to give him one of his less annoying phrases, the one about credit.

'Credit where credit's due, we would never have apprehended those three ecological villains if you hadn't had such sharp eyes. Incidentally, it has been intimated from on high that this should be added to your equipment for the bike.'

He handed Wainwright a small, very sharp knife, usually used for paper-cutting.

'What's this . . .?'

'It's for tyre-slashing. Could be extremely useful if you have to incapacitate some bent bike.'

PC Wainwright thought about it for a moment, then gave it him back.

'Sorry, Sarge. Once you start arming the bobby in the saddle, you're really asking for trouble.'

He walked out into the sunlight, leaving, for once, a dumbstruck Sarge behind him.

(Coming soon – more thrilling adventures of the bobby on the bike!)

Death Begins at Forty

MY six-month-old son had a caller the other day. She asked if she could come in, get him undressed and look him over. I didn't know he knew anyone that well. She turned out to be the health visitor, so she came in and gave him a check-up, questioned his diet and investigated his hand-eye co-ordination – that sort of thing.

We asked if it was normal not to be crawling yet, and she said, yes, many babies skipped that stage and went straight to walking. In fact, some children these days skipped the walking and waited till they could get a moped. She then made some marks on a height-weight graph and prepared to leave.

'No bruises on him, anyway,' she said jokingly, 'so you're probably not beating him up.'

'All the bruises are on me!' I said. 'He doesn't know his own strength. He pulls my hair, nearly twists my ear off . . .'

'These are serious allegations,' said the health visitor, taking her coat off again. 'I'd better examine you.'

It sounds ridiculous, but apparently in some local authorities there are no upper age limits on an examination by a health visitor. To her, I was just a large male child in its forties. She weighed me and measured me. She made marks on a graph. She frowned.

'He's not coming on as well as I would like,' she told my wife. 'We don't like to see too much weight increase at this stage in their development, and I'm a little worried by signs of height shrinkage. What are you giving him to eat?'

My wife described my diet.

'Ugh, no wonder. Try him for a while on plain fish dishes and brown bread. Look for the food packages labelled No Salt, No Sugar, No Pesto, Mayonnaise-Free and No Added Maître d'Hôtel Butter. Is he still taking the bottle?'

'Taking the *bottle*?' I expostulated, but it was as if they could not hear me.

'Yes,' said my wife. 'He gets through quite a lot of a popular red Bulgarian bottle feed.'

'No more of that,' said the health visitor. 'They do a very nice bottled spring water at Fathercare. Try him on that for a couple of months. How's his walking coming along?'

'He's perfectly capable of it, but he doesn't do much. He prefers bicycling.'

'A lazy way of walking. Take his bicycle away from him. Does he have any recreational activity leanings?'

'How do you mean?'

'Well, if you leave him alone, does he cry and grumble, or can he amuse himself?'

'He has his old collection of jazz 78s, which he enjoys. Steam trains he likes. He reads a lot – I think he's getting through his Raymond Chandler again at the moment.'

'Dear, oh dear! Oh dear! Oh dear!' said the health visitor. 'That's painfully retrogressive.'

'And he finds it hard to throw old papers away.'

'Oh dear! Oh dear! OH DEAR! Any signs of competitive sport activity?'

'No.'

'Really? Unexpected sign of maturity there.'

'Look!' I said. Nobody looked.

'How is his mind/hand/eye co-ordination?'

'I don't know. How can you tell?'

'Well, if you ask him to cut the lawn, sort out the bank statements, or fiddle with the car, how well does he do?'

My wife told her.

'Very slow reactions,' she wrote down. 'Abnormally small technical response. Pitifully low motor awareness. Negative financial responsibility.'

'Listen!' I said. Nobody listened.

'Any other hobbies?'

'He likes to switch on things like the BAFTA award ceremonies on television and shout: "Cultural Incest! Rubbish! Smug poseurs!" at the screen.'

'Infantile jealousy,' said the health visitor briskly. She turned to me at last.

'What do you think of the Government's performance, little man?' she said.

'To be frank,' I said, 'I think that the amount of interference into people's daily lives it allows, especially from you, is scandalous. If people want to go down the primrose path of old jazz 78s and Bulgarian Cabernet Sauvignon, they should be allowed to. People want to be left alone, not nannied.'

'Hmm, well, his creeping conservatism and loss of socialist reflexes is pretty much to be expected, I'm afraid. All in all, I'd say he was mentally regressing, subject to horizon shrinkage, physically declining, recreationally ossified and suffering occasional bruises through inept child handling.'

'Is that bad?'

'Not at all,' said the health visitor. 'Absolutely normal at his age. I'll be back in six months for another check.'

I think I'll be out that day.

Can Grass Lead to the Harder Stuff?

SOMETHING is happening in British farming which is so unmentionable and so unbelievable that nobody has yet mentioned it and if they did, nobody would believe it. Only the readers of this column, I like to think, are grown-up enough for the truth, which appears here today for the first time anywhere.

The repeated use of chemicals and pesticides has turned many fields in Britain into drug addicts.

I'll say that again, just in case you didn't grasp it first time round: farmers have put so many chemical additives on their fields that in many cases the fields have become addicted to the chemicals and cannot operate without them.

This information came to me in a top secret memo from the Ministry of Agriculture and Fisheries. Well, most information these days is passed around in the form of highly confidential memos leaked to the press — I get 20 or 30 a day and normally use them as scrap paper — but this one seemed slightly different, so I got in touch immediately with Dr Vernon Barley, a leading farming psychiatrist. He confirmed that it was true.

'You mean, fields can actually show signs of drug addiction?' I asked him.

'Why not?' he said. 'All these chemicals, pesticides, fertilizers and everything are only drugs by other names. They give fields a big buzz. But you have to keep increasing the dose to get the same effect from a field year after year, and by that time your field is a junky.

'I'll give you an example. I'm dealing with a large field in Northamptonshire at the moment — let's call it Ten Acre Meadow, though that's not its real name — which has been on massive amounts of a certain chemical for eight years and has now totally freaked out. It refuses to grow any more crops in meaningful quantities and just sits around pushing up grass all day. Basically, it's hallucinating.'

'How do you mean, hallucinating?'

'It's got delusions of grandeur. It thinks it's Hyde Park.'

Similar delusions are, apparently, quite common. Dr Barley has another field in his care which thinks it is the reincarnation of the Woodstock Festival, and he has come across others which thought they were Bosworth Field, the Field of the Cloth of Gold and some corner of a foreign field. But very often they are too far gone even to have delusions and are just burnt-out wrecks.

'The symptoms tend to vary from town to country. A junky urban field tends to have unsightly bits of concrete, clapped out cars, old bus shelters, lots of rosebay-willow-herb. An addicted rural field is more likely to have abandoned agricultural machinery, old horse jumps and uncontrolled bramble growth.

'But even then you can't be sure, because addicts sometimes get very cunning and lead a double life. Ostensibly they might just be getting on with producing quotas of wheat, but all the time they're craving for more and more fixes of their favourite pesticide. Nobody can lie better than a junky field.'

Dr Barley says that most of East Anglia is now hopelessly addicted, but that there are cases all over the country. His treatment involves taking the field gently out of agriculture and into some other activity like forestry, tourism, theme parks or rock festivals, where commercial chemicals present no temptation. He is delighted that Government policy is now following him.

'You can't really blame the fields for this drug problem. It's the farmers and the Government who have been the dealers and drug pushers, persuading fields to take higher and higher doses of the filthy stuff. Now at last the Government is beginning to see the error of its ways and is using forestry and so on as a rehabilitation treatment.

'The trouble is that even when you get a field off drugs, the stuff is still around in its system for years to come. An organic field which has previously been on chemicals is really a junky underneath; one sack of chemical fertilizer and it would be off again.'

Anyone who thinks he knows a field with problems is advised to get in touch immediately with Fields Anonymous, or to contact Dr Barley's organization, Meadowcare. If it's a field which has recently shed a hedgerow or let a public right of way get overgrown, it almost certainly has problems. Act now before it's too late. There is nothing worse than a field which thinks it can handle its drug problems.

Pedantry United

FOLLOWING my recent observations on pedantry I have received several thousand letters from pedantic readers, most of them objecting to my use of the word 'wrong' as an adverb. My dictionary, however, gives 'wrong' as both an adverb and an adjective, so instead of hurting the feelings of these readers by hurling my dictionary back at them, I am placing all their letters in a time capsule and burying it in my garden for future generations to wonder at, and reply to if they feel like it.

The other letters are more varied. In fact, some of them are worth reprinting, so I am handing this space over to my readers, while I go fishing.

From Doug Pantile

Sir, I wonder which dictionary you refer to for definitions of things like 'wrong'? As a hard-pressed journalist, I have always used what is probably the worst dictionary ever published, the 1986 *Belgian Academy Guide to Pidgin English*. It can be guaranteed to back me up every time, no matter how bad my mistake is. So when people write in to tell me that I have used a word wrong, I simply write back: 'Not according to my dictionary'. This always refutes them (My dictionary gives refute as: 'To tell one fella person to shovel off, to give him a big, bad mouth, to bamfoozle.') Yours etc.

From Mrs Wordy-Montague

Sir, Shall I tell you my least favourite phrase? *[yes – Ed.]* Thanks. My least favourite phrase is: 'He stands somewhere to the right of Genghis Khan'. Not only is this a worn-out cliché, but it is not true, as in many ways Mr Khan was a bit of a reformer. He tried to open a tariff-free area in Europe, he worked wonders with the postal system between Europe and Mongolia, and his enlightened housing policy is still talked about in parts of Dacia. So let's hear no more anti-Khan sentiments. Yours etc.

From Sir Dudley Dwarf

Sir, It makes me furious to hear Khan used as a name. It is, in fact, a title, like Singh or Sir, and means something like Very Important Person, Big Cheese, or Bee's Knees. Yours etc.

From Doug Pantile

Sir, Not according to my dictionary. Yours, etc.

From Gladys Witherington

Sir, Why, oh why, must people use the expression 'bee's knees'? Are children no longer taught the anatomy of insects? Bees do NOT have knees. They have a sort of double-jointed elbow which performs several functions, including pollen-grading, playing dance music and repelling the advances of homosexual bees. But they are NOT knees. Yours etc.

From Henry Whelk

Sir, I wonder how many of your readers are aware that Genghis Khan was a pioneer of cultural internationalism? Finding that many of the tribesmen in his horde did not understand each other, he had a dictionary made of their talk. If anyone ever argued usage with Genghis, he would say: 'Not according to my dictionary', then cut their head off. Yours etc.

From Sir Dudley Dwarf

Sir, Why, oh why, must people insist on using Genghis as if it were a first name? Genghis is in fact a nickname, meaning 'boring, long-winded, as repetitive as the river Ganges'. Let's have no more of this maddening misuse. Yours etc.

From Molly Knutsford, JP

Sir, Aren't we taking pedantry a bit far? If Khan was not a name and Genghis was not a name, what was the poor man called? Honestly, it makes me absolutely furious. Yours etc.

From the Bishop of Wimbledon

Sir, I hope you don't mind my interrupting this little correspondence, but I am one of the bishops who has been asked by Mrs Thatcher to help raise the level of personal morality in this country, and I have been detailed to look after the ethics of public debate. I couldn't help noticing that these jolly interesting letters were getting a little heated, so I am just butting in to say: OK, chaps, cool down! Let's keep violence out of letter-writing, shall we? Right – back to your fascinating discussion! Yours etc.

From Genghis Hutchison

Sir, It may come as surprise to you toffee-nosed lot to learn that Genghis is alive and well as a name. My best friend at school is called Tamburlaine, and there are one or two boys called Kubla and Attila. Any more ill-informed comment, and we might just come round to ravage your homes and leave the landscape a smoking waste, OK?

Also, you don't say 'one of the bishops who has been asked', it's 'one of the bishops who HAVE been asked', Why, oh why, must people make this elementary error? Don't be surprised if your cathedral gets done over this week by a mystery horde which sweeps out of the East and passes across the face of the country like a scourge. Yours etc.

You, the Law and Video (Repeat)

TODAY a well-known lawyer answers your queries about the law.
Q. I wonder if you can help me. The other night I was taking a videotape copy of a movie being shown on BBC 2. Suddenly my French windows burst open and a gang of well-dressed men rushed in and overpowered me. They explained that they were representatives of a film guild which was sick and tired of having their films pirated by members of the public, and they were determined to set an example. They then took £45 off me by force, plus £10 for Michael Caine who apparently has a special arrangement. Can this be right? *BP of Leeds*

A well-known lawyer writes: Unfortunately they are well within their rights, and you are technically in the wrong. That is the law, I am afraid.

Q. I wonder if you can help me. I have a rented video machine with which I can copy films, although of course I would never dream of doing so as it is against the law. Instead, my family, friends and I like to recreate famous movies, doing all the parts ourselves and writing new dialogue.

Well, recently we had just completed a remake of a film starring Michael Caine, and were sitting down to watch it, when a gang of well-dressed businessmen burst in and threw writs at us. Their claim was that by remaking a famous movie, we had infringed over 127 copyright agreements and owed them over £10,000. They then sold off all our furniture and effects to raise the money, and built a new house in our garden to help pay Michael Caine.

Can this be right? *TC of Cardiff*

A well-known lawyer writes: Unfortunately, they are well within their rights and you are technically in the wrong. That is the law, I am afraid.

Q. I wonder if you can help me. I recently hired a video recorder, though not of course for using – I am far too well aware of the risks and legal penalties involved. I simply wanted to have the machine in my sitting room for display.

The 12 months passed without incident (except for a gang of well-dressed men who burst in from time to time, and retired disappointed when they saw my VCR was not plugged in) and I finally asked to have the set taken away. The removal men then pointed out that when I had originally signed the form, I had also signed over possession of the house, garden and everything to them.

I am sure that if I had read the small print I would never have agreed to this, but they said they now had a particularly sharp lawyer working on their contracts and asked me to leave the house at once. Can this be right? *FG of Newquay*

A well-known lawyer writes: This is the law as it stands, I am afraid, and they are perfectly within their rights; there is nothing you can do about it.

Q. I recently befriended a poor chap who, through some legal mix-up, had had his house and everything repossessed by a television rental firm, and was homeless. He and I were standing on the pavement idly watching a programme in the window of a TV rental shop when suddenly we were jostled by a gang of well-dressed businessmen who told us to pay them basic Equity rates for the actors in the film or to move on. We refused, of course, so they fetched a policeman to have us stopped from watching the film, which he did. Can this be right? *CV of Newquay*

A well-known lawyer writes: Sadly, they are well within their rights and you are technically wrong, but that is the law.

Q. I am a policeman who was recently asked to move on a couple of blokes from a TV rental window, and when they asked what they were doing wrong, I told them that the law of England was so complex that at any one time all citizens are breaking at least 10 laws, and I could arrest them for almost anything. Was there any truth in what I said? *Sgt FD of Newquay*

A well-known lawyer writes: Technically you are well within your rights and they are wrong. But that is the law as it stands.

Q. I saw a village well-dressing ceremony recently, and I wondered if that is where the expression 'a well-dressed person' came from. What do you think? *LS of Forest Hill*

A well-known lawyer writes: They are technically within their rights and you are wrong, but that is the law.

The editor of the *Independent* writes: You are a fraud. You are not even reading the readers' queries. You will be sued under the Trades Description Act and fired on the spot.

A well-known lawyer writes: I think not. Read my contract.

A well-known lawyer will be back soon to deal with more of your inquiries.

Grander Than Booker,
Wilder Than Whitbread

STARTING today, the biggest blockbusting novel for years — Book Prize! Book Prize *tells of the powder keg created when four men and women are locked away to choose the novel of the year — and discover that the novels they have read do not contain half the passion that explodes among them. Here is the first dynamite instalment of* Book Prize.

'I liked Will Artley's novel from Australia enormously,' said Enid. 'The feeling of space created by the outback, the almost universal suffering embodied in the crippled boomerang repairman, was so refreshing after the provincialism of most British novels.'

She hadn't actually been able to finish Artley's endless saga, but she wagered shrewdly that none of the others had either.

'Rubbish,' said Peter Abbey. 'What on earth could be more provincial than the Australian desert? We in Britain always assume that anything set in our country is suburban and anything set in a country without street lighting is noble and universal. I shall use my vote to make sure that nothing from Australia wins.'

'Hear, hear,' said Murray, the literary whizz kid from Auckland.

'Or New Zealand,' said Peter.

'Hear, hear,' said Murray, who hated every writer in New Zealand except himself.

'God, I could kill him,' thought Enid, looking at Peter's handsome features, swollen by years of having, well, just one more drink. Peter, the top literary agent in London, was temporarily without an Australian author to represent, which helped to explain his feelings.

Enid herself was a well thought of novelist, that is, one who was hardly thought of at all, either well or badly. She had once had a fleeting affair with Peter which ended abruptly at the Frankfurt Book Fair. It had also started at the Frankfurt Book Fair. It had been very fleeting.

'Look, we haven't even talked about the A N Wilson novel yet,' said Sophie Trimbridge. 'I must say, I rather liked it.'

'Can't give a prize to someone with initials,' said Murray promptly. 'Very old-fashioned, very confusing. For years I thought A S Byatt was a man.'

'For years I thought A N Wilson was a man,' said Peter, and they all laughed except Enid, who said: 'But he is a man.'

'It's a joke, dear,' said Peter, patting her on a hand which was promptly pulled away. Enid looked quickly over to Sophie Trimbridge for unspoken support but Sophie, as usual, was putting her hair in place. Sophie ran a highly regarded television books programme, which meant that it was well thought of but not actually regarded by anyone. To her surprise, Enid got a flashing smile of support, not from Sophie, but from the New Zealander, Murray. She smiled gratefully back. She rather liked the look of Murray who, though only the writer of one novel, was much sought after by the BBC, even if seldom found, as he was usually in the pub.

'I think we have to be sensible about this,' said Murray. 'I think we have to vote for a readable novel, I think we have to vote for a writer who is already respected, and I think we have to vote for a woman, as men have won it for two years running.'

'I think you're talking like a pompous, self-elected chairman,' said Peter. Murray got up. Enid thought for a moment he was going to hit Peter.

'I think it's time for a little drink,' said Murray, ignoring Peter and passing through into the small inner room where the hospitality was kept. Enid went to stand by the window, staring out at the London rooftops. To her horror, she felt Peter come up behind her.

'I often think of Frankfurt,' said his voice in her ear. Enid, who also thought of Frankfurt but only with disgust, broke away and ran into the inner room to find some sanity. There, to her increasing horror, she saw Murray deep in an embrace with Sophie Trimbridge, their mouths joined as if both were playing each other like trumpets. They did not notice her. She returned to the main room. Peter grinned.

'I've noticed you making eyes at the little Kiwi. Well, I'm afraid he fancies poor old Sophie, not you. You'll have to make do with me.'

He advanced towards her. Instinctively she picket up the new Iris Murdoch and threw it at him. It was a surprisingly good shot, catching him on the temple and sending him sliding senseless to the floor.

Should she have thrown something lighter, like an Anita Brookner? Has she really killed a fellow judge? And if Peter recovers, will he get his evil way? Don't miss the next exciting instalment of Book Prize!

The Winter Olympics Explained

BAFFLED by the strange events in the Winter Olympics? Unable to tell a slalom from a jeroboam? Puzzle no longer, with this easy-to-tear-out-and-ruin-the-article-on-the-other-side-of-the-page supplement.

DOWNHILL SKI JUMP

In the countries of the north skiing is not just a sport but a means of travel. And one of the hazards the lone skier must face in the vast forests is suddenly finding in his path a huge ramp down which he must slide, then jump off, glide to a halt, take off his goggles and stare back in frustrated disbelief at the giant electronic scoreboard hidden in the depths of the mighty pines. Possibly the hardest event of all. Watch out for the giant Swiss, Piggi Goggelbach.

ALPINE GOGGLE RACE

The inhabitants of Austria, Sweden and the other northern countries have always ski'd vast distances wearing a swimming cap, goggles, mask and nothing else, except a body stocking of rubber bearing advertising. In this, perhaps the hardest of all events, the entrants have to gather after the finish and guess who each other is. Watch out for the charismatic Swede Inge Puddle — or is it the fearsome Austrian Franz Dimanche? Do they know themselves?

CROSS-COUNTRY ICE DANCING

The countries of the north, from Russia to Norway, are linked by a series of high, icy tracks down which the inhabitants dance at an amazing rate – 3.5 kilometres per bolero is considered a good cruising speed – though they must halt from time to time to change the Ravel or Soft Machine tape on their portable cassette recorder, or repair any rent in their high-sheen Durex protective clothing. The hardest ordeal of all? Perhaps. Watch for the resurgent Norwegian, Zuggi Skvint.

DOWNHILL CAUCUS

This American speciality comes top in the toughness stakes. It may seem complicated to our eyes, but it's quite simple. In snowtime, groups of American voters get together in caucuses to select delegates. These delegates later meet to elect an electoral college. The college then chooses a candidate. The candidate then enters the race. Too late, unfortunately, as the race was over six months ago. Watch out for falling American superstar Grog Pizzle.

UPHILL SKI DANCING

In doubtless the hardest of all events, the contestants have to progress uphill wearing heavy skis and full evening dress, keeping strict time to an old cracked record of a Strauss waltz, as their Nordic ancestors did long ago rather than go out and see the new Ibsen play. It's toughest in summer when there's no snow. Keep an eye open for lovely Austrian couple Kurt and Lady Waldheim, doing their routine to 'It's A Sin To Tell A Lie'.

UNMANNED BOBSLEIGH

The hardest event of all? Well, it's so risky, with maximum speeds of 700 mph, that this year no contestants have been allowed and only stuffed dummies are on board. The bob takes corners at nearly 500 mph, holds the road very well but doesn't really have enough luggage space and the suspension is primitive. At that price, I'd go for a Porsche or BMW. Watch out for the announcer; he might be British, at least.

NORDIC CROSS-COUNTRY ICE HOCKEY

Did you know that years ago the people of the north suddenly had mad fits in which they set off through the forest, knocking over red flags, crouching so low their bottoms burst into flame on contact and whacking a small puck or each other? The winner was the first country to invade Finland. Now, this little-changed game is probably the toughest in the Olympiad and certainly the hardest to understand. Watch out for petite Danish masseuse, Dinky Mekkano. I met her in Sarajevo, and she's a bundle of fun.

APRES MOI LE LUGE

So said Louis XIV, and it certainly looks as if it were invented by a French monarch with no engineering training. The four contestants jump on the luge and vanish at about 75 mph, which suits us fine. Watch out for the wacky Norwegian quartet Grocko, Horpo, Chiko and Gmo.

MARDI GRASS SKIING

Right across the lands of the north, life is governed by ice, snow and the great forest, but in the south it is a different matter. For here they have carnival. Yes, the passionate heat of the samba, the luscious curve of dark flesh, the strange call of the blood and the blinding costumes – all this is worlds away from the vaulted northern forests. Stark, icy beauty . . . hot midday madness . . . is there no middle way between these two great cultures?

There is, actually. You can go to Britain instead and watch housewives trotting along holding pancakes.

It's Your Line and Their Call

TODAY I have a message of hope for British Telecom. I have identified an area in which thousands of millions of pounds are being wasted on the telephone each year, and it is all our fault, not BT's. This scandalous wastage occurs every time we ring up someone who has a domestic partner in the offing.

Does this sound mysterious? Well, consider the following scenario and see if it rings any bells. Let us say that you are called Peter and you have just rung your Uncle Robert to know if you can stay the night next week, when business takes you in his vicinity. The conversation starts like this . . . **Uncle:** Peter! How lovely to hear from you! How are you and Anna?

You: We're fine. Anna's much better after her rock-climbing incident. And how's Aunt Betty?

Uncle: Oh, fine, considering the drinking. Anyway, to what do we owe the honour?

You: Well, I'll be down your way next Tuesday on business and wondered if there was any chance of a bed for the night . . .

Uncle: Of course, old chap . . . It's Peter.

Why has he suddenly announced that it's Peter, a fact well known to both of you? Because, of course, Aunt Betty has just come into the room at their end. She wants to know who Uncle is talking to. He tells her. Does she now leave him in peace? Not a chance. The scenario continues thus.

Aunt: (indistinctly) Gooby goo?

Uncle: He's fine.

Aunt: Gooby Anna?

Uncle: Fine. Her broken legs are mending well.

Aunt: Oh, good. Gooby gooble Peter?

Uncle: He's looking for a bed next week.

Aunt: Goodle?

Uncle: Tuesday.

Aunt: Goosday? Goodle gobble gribble Actons!

Uncle: The Actons? Oh, God. You never told me we were having dinner with the Actons on Tuesday.

Anyone recognize this little playlet? Good. Now answer two simple questions. From the time Aunt Betty enters the room: a) who does all the talking?; b) who pays for the call? That's right. Your aunt and uncle are talking about you at your expense. Now they forget you altogether.

70

Aunt: I told you last week we had fixed dinner with the Actons.
Uncle: I don't remember.
Aunt: Well, it doesn't matter. Peter can come to dinner as well. I'm sure he'd love that.
Uncle: I don't think he actually likes the Actons. I know *I* don't.
Aunt: Oh God, you're being difficult again.
Uncle: No, I'm not. I'm simply . . .

Do you see what has happened? They are now having one of their arguments. You can't hear quite what it's about and yet you're paying.

Of course, you cannot be indefinitely excluded. Sooner or later you are brought back into the conversation, but it is not in a way you really welcome. It involves Aunt Betty suddenly taking over the phone . . .

Aunt: Oh, let me talk to him! . . . Hello, Peter! How are you?
You: I'm fine, Aunt Betty. How are you?
Aunt: Never felt better in all my life, except in the mornings. How's Anna?
You: Fine, except that the twins keep putting graffiti on the plaster on her broken legs.
Aunt: You must thank her for the lovely letter she sent us.
Note: female relatives are much better than men at thanking you for letters sent. Much better at sending them, too. For instance, you probably will not even pass Aunt's thanks on to Anna. Anyway, what we have now is a further reprise of the conversation, interrupted only by a further ghastly development. The deposed uncle starts a come-back.
Uncle: Gooby goo goo?
Aunt: Hold on, Peter . . . What's that, Robert? I don't know what kind of car he'll be driving – does it matter?
Uncle: Goobly gosh goodle.
Aun: Why can't we take the Volvo?
Uncle: Goodle gosh all goodle.
Aunt: You're fixed for it to be serviced! *When?*
Uncle: Geb Goosday.
Aunt: Oh, heaven save us!

At the end of 20 minutes you have probably had two minutes' conversation yourself, and you have paid for all the 18 minutes during which your uncle and aunt were having a lively private discussion of life. This is wasting money on a scale to which BT has not yet aspired.

Still, look on the bright side. It's probably the only decent conversation your uncle and aunt have had all evening. If you hadn't rung, they might nor even have spoken to each other. And at least Anna didn't join in at your end.

71

Autumn — Everything Must Go

AUTUMN! All over the country the leaves turned green, then amber, then red, and came to a confused halt. Flocks of Aston Martins gathered twittering in the outskirts of cities, then fled for warmer climes. A government spokesman confirmed the trend.

'I welcome this trend into the Church of England,' he intoned. 'May it grow until it becomes a fully fledged fact.'

Autumn! House prices fluttered in the South-east, rose slightly in the North-west and eased down comfortably in East Anglia. A band of hot air came in off the Irish Sea and settled over the Labour Party in Blackpool. All over the country, leaves turned four glorious colours — strawberry, coffee, chocolate and pistachio — and fell softly on to the wafer-brown fields. The M25 slowly circled London and came to a complete stop somewhere near Staines.

> 'Tis as I feared, The old man's beard
> Has turned my hedge to something weird,

hummed the farmer to himself, as clouds of seagulls eddied and flowed behind his tractor. In Brussels, hawk-eyed Eurocrats slapped an extra £5 per tonne on seagull production, while in Somerset the basket-weavers put aside their half-finished baskets and turned to the mass production of hockey sticks in anticipation of a post-Olympic hockey craze. Snap! The withies are broken off at 4 ft high. Crackle! They are curved gently over a fire and wrapped with rubber handing. Pop! They are applied with vigour to the fragile ankles of opponents just outside the penalty area . . .

Snap, crackle, pop — in the cereal fields of England, vast expanses of Rice Krispies and Sugar Puffs ripen in the late sun and are harvested into huge cardboard boxes. Slap, tickle, soap — the TV autumn schedules spread thinly across the land and fall to earth in a mist of *déjà vu*. Rap, tinkle, crap — the Top Twenty twitters from a thousand jeans shops as the shop-lifter goes about his trade, gently lifting piles of denim to find his correct leg-size . . .

Autumn! In the fields, a youthful nature-spotter pulls his father's sleeve and says: 'Look, Dad, isn't that the Common Agricultural Policy?' The sunlight falls on old St Paul's, knee-deep in ice cream wrappers by Walls, while in gardens everywhere barbecue kits and lawn mowers gather for the annual migration to the garden shed.

Autumn! The leaves on the trees turn three award-winning shades of gold, silver and bronze. A plump chestnut, its fruit rippling brown in the golden sunshine, is disqualified for taking steroids and banned for three years by the International Conker Committee. In the room the women come and go, talking of little Michael and Jello. A hundred years of Eliot, and nothing much to show, but a bunch of collected lettuce, where the poems used to grow.

Autumn! Comedians turn blue, Mary Whitehouse turns puce and Dick Whittington turns again, ready for the new panto season. April is the cruellest month, but October tortures the trees till the leaves turn blue, brown and black in the face, then expire. The tourists gather in Gatwick, and huddle in Heathrow, ready for the long migration back to Cincinnati and Minneapolis. But how exactly do you spell Cincinnati and Minneapolis? Yes, it's the new autumn season of Mastermind, and you are going to answer questions on your special subject, which is . . .?

Autumn! Who wrote 'Autumn Leaves'? What is the special autumn number? If winter comes, can spring be furbelow? When shall we three meet again, in gently falling English rain? Australian lager flows down the drain, in dark brown pools of Castlemaine. The leaves on the trees turn four exciting flavours of smoky bacon, Bovril, roast chicken and hedgehog, before crunching on the field below like a giant, crumpled crisp packet . . .

Autumn! Down to the last six entrants in the Booker Prize, and the judges prod and poke the half dozen fat novels as they parade round the paddock. Later they will be slaughtered and packed in paperback for quick Christmas consumption, but just for the moment they are kings of the ring. Ring ring . . . ring ring . . . someone is on the line to Kingsley Amis for his annual article on how to deal with Christmas hangovers. But there is no cure for hangovers and there is no cure for . . .

Autumn! An irreversible downward drift of shares in three shades of gilt, blue chip and congold. A gentle fall of seasonally adjusted figures . . . A thick layer of yellowing paperwork . . . A soft rain falling on the just and the unjust, the nearly and the not quite . . .

Autumn. Coming to your neighbourhood soon.

The Nuclear Wastelands of Time

Today: A complete science fiction story!
THERE is a certain place where pure science and industry meet. Sometimes it is called industrial research; sometimes it's known as business funding; in the case of Professor Frewd and Boris Nutting, it was the saloon bar of the Antelope Arms.

Boris Nutting was one of the brightest young men in the nuclear fuel business (at university, he had infuriated his fellow students with a car sticker: 'Nuclear Energy? Yes, please!'). Professor Frewd, 20 years older, was the laconic head of Sellafield University, set up in 1995 to accelerate nuclear research in the so-called Leak District. It was said that behind his impersonal façade, Professor Frewd led a happy home life with his wife and children, but nothing had ever been proved.

'Why here?' said Frewd.

'It's the only safe place,' said Boris. 'Here we can't be overheard.'

'What?' shouted Frewd, over the jukebox. They wandered out into the fresh air, it being one of those rare days when you can be outside in Britain without your beer freezing. They stood and looked over the rolling hills, dales and power stations of old England.

'I wanted to get hold of you because I have had a revolutionary idea and you're the only person I dare try it out on.'

'Try away,' said Frewd.

'Whatever problems we have in creating nuclear energy, the biggest at the end of the day is disposal of waste. I mean, it's not a big problem in practical terms. Practically, we can just dump it or bury it. But in public relation terms, we have a giant headache.'

'Agreed,' said Frewd. But what he was thinking was, wasn't Boris a funny name for a top British scientist?

'Now here's my revolutionary idea. Why do we have to bury nuclear waste in another place? *Why can't we bury it in another time?*'

'Sorry?' said Frewd, as well he might.

'There are constant rumours that one government department – nobody knows which – has made the vital break-through into time travel. They say it is being used for diplomatic purposes only, at the moment – I've heard people say that we are travelling back in time to try to stop Truman dropping the bomb. Also forward to steal Japanese industrial secrets.'

'Uh huh,' said Frewd.

74

'Well, why don't we explore the possibilities of using time travel to take our waste to another age and get rid of it there? If the technology exists, let's try it while we've got the chance. Before ecology starts respecting other ages as well as other places.'

Professor Frewd stared into his pint. Boris looked at him, thinking what a strange name Frewd was. Welsh? American? German dialect? Then Frewd sighed and spoke.

'It's been tried already.'

'It's what?'

'We were the department that got time travel together in the first place, for the very aim you suggest. We went ahead and buried all our nuclear waste in another part of history. Very convenient, very easy. What we had forgotten was that it was possible to contaminate and spread disease in other parts of history as well.'

'Like how?' It was Boris's turn for the terse role.

'We opted for the Middle Ages. We reckoned it was a period that nobody was too much in love with. Unfortunately, we caused an epidemic.'

'I can't believe that. Surely we'd know about it if it had happened.'

'We do. It's called the Black Death.'

'*You* caused the Black Death?'

Professor Frewd nodded. They both stared into space for a while.

'You could try burying it in the future,' offered Boris.

'Oh, we have, we have. We've buried some contaminated waste on 16 July 2043, at 3 pm.

'Unfortunately, that went a bit wrong as well. But at least we know that when that date and time comes, we can be there ready to stop the waste being buried. By force, if necessary.'

'You mean, in 40 years' time we'll be repelling our own invasion? You, as an old man, will meet yourself as a young man and try to shoot him? But . . .'

The implications were enormous. Too enormous.

'Tell me one thing,' said Boris. 'Where does the name Frewd come from?'

'Austria. It's a civil service misprint for Freud. And Boris?'

'My mother desperately wanted a daughter. She was going to call her Doris. This was the nearest she could get.'

It made sense. As much as anything made sense these days.

1992 and the English Language

I FOUND myself chatting in the train the other day to a distinguished-looking if somewhat pompous and long-winded man (rather luckily, because I had left a distinguished-looking if somewhat pompous and long-winded at paperback at home by mistake) and at one point he was adumbrating a theory about the future of Europe. Adumbrating is the sort of word he liked.

'I find it hard to lend credence to that,' I said. The style was catching. He smiled secretly to himself.

'You will find it impossible in a year or two,' he murmured.

'Pardon?' I said. 'You were murmuring.'

'You will find it impossible to lend credence to anything in a year or two,' he said loudly. 'The expression will be illegal.'

Seeing my total incomprehension, he took it on himself to explain that the government department in which he works is planning to phase out all non-profit-making and unproductive phrases between now and 1992, and to make the English language streamlined and efficient.

'So what is inefficient about "lending credence"?' I asked.

'It is an inefficient way of saying "believe". Worse than that, we never use the word "credence" without using the word "lend" as well. People never borrow credence, or donate it, or set credence up in trust for their children. They just lend it. We are determined to stamp out all one-use words.'

What he meant, it turned out, was that there are many words in English which are only used in one context. If these were all eliminated, the savings would be enormous. So he claimed. I demanded examples.

'Well, "stiff as a ramrod" and "plain as a pikestaff" are two good ones. We never use the words "ramrod" or "pikestaff" otherwise. We have never seen a pikestaff or a ramrod, and I doubt if we would recognize one if we did.'

'But they are picturesque and colourful phrases,' I objected. 'The language would be the poorer without them.'

'Twaddle,' said the man. 'You don't even know why we say them. Why don't we say "plain as a ramrod" or "stiff as a pikestaff"? Makes just as good sense. But we don't even bother to think what we're saying. When we eliminate these one-use words, we are rooting out pernicious clichés. We are clearing away the ground elder and couch grass of language!'

'Tell me some more words due for the compost heap,' I said. He pulled out a list and consulted it.

'"Nether" – only used of regions. "Bated" – happens only to breath. "Bearding" – something done only to a lion. "Bald" – only word used with pate . . .'

'You can't get rid of "bald"!' I expostulated.

'It's "pate" we're getting rid of,' he explained patiently. 'Battening down hatches. Wringing of withers. Figment of the imagination. A palpable hit. A dab hand. Short shrift. . .'

'Do you mean to say,' I said slowly, 'that these words are never used in any other context? Not ever?'

'Absolutely,' he said. '"Dab" is never used as an adjective apart from "hand". When did you last commend someone as a dab foot, or dab eye, or dab pectoral muscle? Have you recently battened down a lid? Given somebody long shrift? Had a palpable miss? Do you even know what dab means, or how you batten hatches down?'

'No,' I said, 'but these phrases have always stood me in good stead.'

'That's another one!' he said triumphantly. 'Good stead, indeed. What is a bad stead? What is a tolerably reasonable stead? Would you know a stead that had failed its MoT test? *Do you even know what a stead is?*'

'Something attached to a bed?' I suggested, but he was off again by then.

'Foregone conclusion. Scotching the rumour. Running amuck. Blot on the escutcheon. Brooking no delay. Venting spleen. Scant regard. Ye olde. Scantily clad. Scurvy knave . . .'

'Hold on, hold on. You can vent wrath as well as spleen.'

'It's "spleen" we're banning. "Vent" just escaped the chop, precisely because of "wrath".'

'Are you banning "ye" or "olde?"'

'Both. They're both pests. If only someone had coined some nice phrases over the years like "Ye Newe Café" or "Ye Bigge Car Parke", we might have spared them, but as it is, they are eroded beyond hope.'

'You said "brooking no delay". You can also brook no opposition.'

There was a long pause. Slowly he crossed it off his list.

'All right. We'll keep "brook" as a verb.'

At least I can say that I personally have saved the life of one English word this week. But there is still a lot of rescue work to be done before 1992.

Bertrand's Mind Wins over Mater

I AM told that there is an enormous demand for children's stories with intellectual rigour as well as an exciting story, so I have devised a series based on famous thinkers of the past, which I am convinced will make my fortune. The first one, which I bring you today, is called:
BERTRAND RUSSELL AND THE BIG RED DUSTBIN.

It was a cold, snowy day in 1888, and all Bertrand wanted to do was stay indoors and think about things. But his mother had other ideas.

'Bertie!' she cried. 'Bertie? Oh, where can he have got to? He seems to have vanished.'

'How many times must I tell you, mother,' said Bertie, appearing behind her, 'that there is no such thing as vanishing? A person cannot dematerialize. Matter is indestructible. So is Mater, come to that,' added Bertie, making one of his rare jokes.

'What about your Uncle George?' said Bertie's mother, who liked nothing better than a rousing philosophical debate. 'He vanished five years ago. So did half the family silver.'

'You are using the word "vanish" in a very loose sense, mother,' said young Bertie, loftily. 'Uncle George merely took a passage to Australia, presumably accompanied by the silver.'

'How did you know that?' said his mother, genuinely surprised. 'Even the police could not trace him.'

'I took the precaution of checking the passenger lists on boats bound for Australia. He was listed as Albert Prince. It was an old joke of his.'

'Why didn't you tell us that?'

'Nobody listens to a five-year-old child on police matters,' said Bertie. 'And now if you don't mind, I've got some thinking to do.'

'Oh no, you don't,' said Bertie's mother. 'I've got a job for you. I want you to take the big red dustbin down to the end of the drive ready for collection by the dustmen.'

'Why should I . . .?'

'Just do it and don't answer back,' said his mother, giving him a clip round the ear-hole.

Young Bertie reddened and tears came to his eyes. This was for two reasons, he quickly analysed. One, because it was shameful to have a mother who was so quick to forget modern educational theory as to substitute physical coercion for sweet reason. Two, because it bloody well hurt. Well, he would get his own back, that he would.

No, no, he thought hastily, petty revenge is NOT the answer. That was as illogical a primitive reaction as his mother's box on the ears had been. If he could not rise above the behaviour of his mother and act logically at all times, what chance of progress was there?

'Bertie!' said his mother crossly, coming back into the room. 'Take that dustbin out before the dustmen come, for God's sake!'

'I hardly think that an appeal to a non-existent deity will have much effect,' said Bertie, with dignity. 'I believe in the existence of the dustmen, yes. The big dustbin, yes. But God, no.'

Another box descended on his ear. Right, thought Bertie grimly. Petty revenge it is, then.

He put on scarf and gloves and went outside into the cold. There stood the big red dustbin in the yard, full of rubbish. Take it down to the road, his mother had said. Right, he would take the dustbin to the road. But he would leave the rubbish behind at the house. That would serve his mother right for not issuing a logical order.

As he was emptying the bin on to the ground, he realized a tramp was standing a few yards away, watching him.

'Having a good time, son?'

Bertie explained briefly the reasoning behind his actions. The tramp nodded approvingly.

'Matter of fact, I need an empty bin myself,' he said, 'so this will come in handy. I also need all the stuff that's on the dining-room dresser. Nip in and get it, there's a good boy.'

Bertie went to fetch the rest of the family silver and put it in the big red dustbin.

'How was Australia, Uncle George?' he said

The tramp smiled.

'Still, the clever one, eh, Bertie? Well, Australia's very expensive, hence my reappearance. But I did remember to bring you a present.'

He gave Bertie a boomerang stamped *Australia Centennial – 100 Years Old*, winked and went off down the drive with the bin on his back. 'Did you take the big red dustbin down to the road?' said his mother later.

'Mother, I promised the bin would be taken down the drive, and it was,' said Bertie, phrasing his sentence to avoid lying. Logic, he had already realized, was the most important thing in the world. After getting your own back, of course.

Coming Soon: Wittgenstein Goes to the Supermarket and Naughty Little Nietzsche.

Is There a Camera in the House?

MPs ARE sometimes portrayed as shrinking violets who want to keep the cameras out of the Commons because they know nothing about television and are nervous of it. One second's thought should dispel this ridiculous idea. No body of people knows TV better at close hand than our MPs. They are on television the whole time. Is there any MP who has not been in the studios? I doubt it.

No, the reason they have always feared having the cameras in the House is that they have had too MUCH experience of television, and they are afraid that *Today in the House* will go something like this . . .

Brian Blister (Marginside, Labour): I consider furthermore that this piece of legislation is the most pernicious, the most repressive, the most pusillanimous and paltry attempt to apply a muzzle to the media which even this government . . .

Floor Manager: I'm sorry, we're not getting you.

Blister: Pardon?

FM: The gallery tells me that there's no sound coming through. Are you switched on?

Blister: No, I'm not. You're right. Sorry.

FM: OK, let's go again from just before there, where you were doing all those adjectives beginning with P, and by the way, try not to pop on them all. And the rest of you! Can we have a bit more spontaneous reaction, please? Let's show the folks at home that we're all having a good time, right? Right. Action.

Blister: I consider this piece of legislation to be the most pernicious, the most putrid . . .

FM: Stop it there for a moment. It's not putrid.

Blister: Yes, it is.

FM: No, it's not, it's repressive, it's pusillanimous . . . You said so first time. You've got to keep that. Otherwise it won't edit.

Blister: I see. All right . . . I consider this legislation to be the most pernicious, the most repressive, the most pusillanimous and . . .

FM: I'm sorry, love. I'll have to stop you there again. You're sweating a lot.

Blister: Well, it's normal to sweat a lot when you think about this government.

FM: Yes, fair enough, nice one, but the gallery tells me we're getting a lot of shine. Could we have Gloria, please?

80

James Shire (Lymeswold, Tory): On a point of information, Mr Speaker, may we know who Gloria is?

Speaker: Gloria is the make-up girl. I believe it is her task to apply small amounts of powder to honourable members when they are wet.

Shire: Then could you request her to apply large amounts of powder to the Tory back-benches? (*Loud, raucous laughter.*)

FM: OK, let's go for another take.

Shire: On a point of information, Mr Speaker, who is Gloria?

FM: No, we're not using that. From 'I consider this piece of legislation . . .' etc. OK, action.

Blister: I consider this piece of legislation to be the most pernicious, the most repressive, the most pusillanimous and paltry attempt to muzzle the media that any government . . .

FM: Brian, love these are your words, and this is your speech, but the gallery just wants to know if all those adjectives are strictly necessary. When it comes to editing, don't forget, the longest sentences go first. Could you just make it putrid and paltry?

Donald Merger (Cornish Isles, SDP): On a point of order, Mr Speaker . . .?

Speaker: Yes?

Merger: I'm sweating a lot. Could I have Gloria?

Speaker: No, you cannot. Carry on, please.

Blister: This piece of legislation is the most paltry, the most putrid attempt to muzzle . . .

Sound recordist: Aeroplane.

FM: Damn. Well, we'll just have to stop again.

Speaker: May I inquire why?

FM: There'll be an aeroplane going over in a minute. The sound man always hears it first.

Blister: But I'm in the very last paragraph of my speech! It won't take a moment.

FM: OK, we'll go for it. Quiet, everybody. QUIET!!

Blister: I consider this to be the most paltry and putrid attempt to muzzle the media that this government has ever attempted. I therefore intend to vote against the . . . the . . . I'm sorry, I've forgotten what Bill we are discussing. (*Outbreak of government cheers and boos.*)

FM: Loves, I think we're all getting a bit tired and frazzled. Let's try again after lunch, in an hour's time, shall we? We'll try from pernicious and putrid again then. All right?

Speaker: May I just say that we have been discussing the same Bill now for over five months. How much longer are we going to be?

FM: As long as it takes, love. This is television now, you know.

The 4-Star Art of Filling Time

WHAT is the most useless thing in the world?

For a long time scientists thought it was the art of pub conversation, but now they are convinced that it may be the time spent filling your car with petrol. For about a minute and a half, you are forced to stand holding a pump in a little hole in your car, the lethal fumes of fuel wafting round your nostrils, and it seems to be the longest time in the world.

'That's because you can't do anything else at the same time,' says Dr Rudolf Differential, a motorway behaviourist. 'Also, because your family is chatting away inside the car and you can't hear a word they say. And also, your pump always seems much slower than anyone else's. In the 90 seconds it takes, you can become depressive, manic, subject to persecution feelings and asphyxiated.'

But it's the sign of a great man that he can make use of the unusable, and I've been ringing round a few celebrities to see how they get through those 90 seconds.

David Owen: 'When I'm filling my car at a petrol station, I usually find it gives me time to start a new political party, with me as leader. Then, when we're ready to go off again, I resign and leave it.'

Jeffrey Archer: 'When I'm filling my car with petrol, I usually write a new play or novel. Sometimes I have a bit of time left over, so I sign autographs. Nowadays I always take my wife with me as a witness.'

Nigel Lawson: 'I stand there watching the little figures flashing round on the dial and I think, blimey, doesn't the money mount up? Then I find I've been watching the litres instead of the pounds, and I think, silly old me. Then, when the pump has switched itself off, I try to get even more petrol into the little hole but usually I just spill it on my trousers.'

One man I met, a yuppie estate agent called Jeremy, says that any moment wasted is a fiver lost, so while he is filling up with petrol he always makes a call on his cordless phone.

'Know what the snag there is?' he says. 'Snag is, I then find myself wasting more time waiting for the number to ring. So, during that space, I turn on my wrist radio to catch up with the news. There again, the radio takes 10 seconds to warm up, so during that time I give myself a complete medical check-up with this little kit here. On a good day, I get the news, my telephone number, a kidney update and petrol on my turn-ups *all at the very same time*.'

Since the start of this article, I have had several angry phone calls protesting about my condemnation of pub conversation as the most boring thing in the world. In fact, one caller says triumphantly that he actually uses the time spent filling his car to *have* a pub conversation.

'As soon as the car's short of fuel, me and a few of the lads pile in and tool down the motorway, know what I mean? Couple of crates of lager in the back, can't be bad, can't be bad. When the little red light goes on, we pull into a service area and fill her up, and during that 90 seconds or so we have a bevvy or two, pull a couple of birds, have a sing-song round the old joanna and get really legless. After that, I can't remember what happens, catch my drift, stone the crows, blimey, I shouldn't wonder . . .'

It's very easy, of course, to forget the other side in all this, the family members – usually women and children – who have to sit inside the car during petrol stops, who never know if their menfolk have enough money for the fuel, if they are going to start an affair with a female motorist while queueing to pay or, worst of all, be tempted to buy a piece of garden furniture at the cash desk.

One of the most tragic cases is of a woman whose husband got out of a blue Escort to fill it up and never came back. Ten weeks later she is still there.

'My solicitor told me that I would be on safer legal grounds for a divorce if I didn't leave the scene of the desertion,' she told me. 'Life in a motorway service area is excruciatingly boring, though I've developed quite a taste for tandoori-flavoured crisps and I see a lot of my friends passing through. I'm also developing a quite pleasant relationship with a lorry driver from Salford who comes through three times a week.'

Well, that just about wraps up the problems of petrol-filling. Personally, I just stare into space. The thing that gets me is queueing to pay for the petrol – I don't mind telling you that I've just written this article standing behind a man who is having immense trouble with his Barclaycard, and now wants his petrol and his extra strong mints put on separate bills for VAT purposes. Blimey – now he's suddenly decided to buy a garden barbeque kit. God give me strength.

Night of the Mole Hunters

'I HAVE reason to believe that there is a mole in the Neighbourhood Watch,' said the Colonel strictly, looking round the meeting.

A mole! In the Neighbourhood Watch! The very idea! It was like saying that there was a Russian agent in the Royal Family. They all looked round suspiciously at each other.

'I'm afraid it's the only theory that makes sense,' continued the Colonel. 'Look, we all pool information about our movements so that we can keep an eye on each other's houses when we're out, and what happens? We've all been burgled!

'That suggests only one thing to me – that one of our number is a criminal who has joined the Neighbourhood Watch to get inside information.'

They knew it made sense. One of them must be the guilty party. They knew it must be so, because they had all read the kind of novel in which all the suspects were gathered together in the library. But who could it be?

They all looked so eminently respectable, from the vicar to Dr Peabody, from old Mrs Treadgold to Professor Brindle. The only one who might conceivably be capable of such a dastardly deed was . . .

'Simon Pullar!' said the Colonel.

'Yes?' said Simon, startled.

'You're the obvious suspect,' said the Colonel. 'You haven't got a job. You lounge around all day, and you only shave once a week. You smoke and drink too much and you wear the most dreadful ties.

'What clinches the matter, to my mind, is that you are the only one who hasn't been burgled.'

Now that the Colonel had pointed it out, it was obvious. Simon Pullar was an untrustworthy layabout, and the only reason he had been admitted to the scheme at all was that he had the remnants of a posh accent.

As the final chapters of Agatha Christie novels went, this was going to be a short one. They might as well take him out and lynch him now.

'Just a moment,' said Simon. 'I think you're all being a little premature. For a start, the reason I haven't been burgled is that I haven't been out of my house. I don't shave because I have a sensitive skin condition. I lounge around all day because my job keeps me at home.'

'What do you *do*?' said the vicar.

'I write detective stories,' said Simon. 'For this purpose I like to find out the personal details of my neighbours and use them as characters, and I must say I've found some *very* interesting things about you lot. For instance, would you be surprised to learn that the professor is not really a professor at all?'

'Nonsense,' said Brindle. 'I go to the university every day.'

'Yes, but your department was closed down last year. You daren't admit it, so you pretend to be employed.

'The doctor is a genuine doctor, but he has a drug addiction problem which is bankrupting him. The colonel is in trouble because he was discharged from the Army under dishonourable circumstances and gets no pension. The vicar . . .'

They all looked at each other furtively. This wasn't how the last chapter was meant to go. It turned out that they all had frightful secrets, nobody more so than Mrs Peabody who had killed her sister to get her inheritance; all except Simon Pullar himself.

The comfy little middle class village had turned out to be a diseased bed of bourgeois depravity.

'Are you trying to say that you are the only one who *isn't* a suspect?' said the Colonel defiantly.

'Not at all,' said Simon. 'For all you know, I might be such a bad detective story writer that I need the money badly enough to do some burgling.'

'Yes, tell us something you've written!' said the doctor, surreptitiously sniffing a little cocaine.

'Well, I've written this story for a start,' said Simon.

'If you're writing this story and we're all characters you've invented,' said the professor slowly, 'that can only mean two things. One, you have some terrible grudge against the middle classes. Two, you must know who the burglar really is.'

'I do,' said Simon. 'He is the man you've all forgotten about. The man who is not a member of the Neighbourhood Watch, but who comes to all our meetings. The man who said he would be along later this evening.'

As he spoke, the door opened and a latecomer entered.

'Sorry I couldn't make it earlier,' said Police Constable Wheelwright. 'Haven't missed anything important have I?'

The Celestial Greenhouse Part One

BEGINNING today, a great new science fiction serial: The Graffiti Effect.

'Good God,' said Professor Greenloft, staring through the biggest telescope in the world. 'I don't believe it.' He looked again. It was still there. 'Good God, said Professor Greenloft, as if repeating it would make it go away. 'I don't believe it.' But it was still there.

The time was 4 am in July, and Professor Greenloft was not even feeling tired. Astronomers, like burglars and jazz musicians, operate best at night, and Professor Greenloft was no exception. He worked from dusk to dawn, putting in much longer hours in midwinter than he did in midsummer to catch the stars at work. His resulting erratic work pattern looked very odd on his PAYE form. The Inland Revenue gave him such a hard time about it that he sometimes thought of going self-employed like jazz musicians, or even entering the black economy with the burglars.

So it was not tiredness that made him see, as he looked through his telescope into the depths of the universe, a tiny message written among the stars: Mars for the Martians.

He went through the usual checks. He made sure that nobody had scribbled something on the lens. He made sure that the eyepiece was not faulty. He made sure that he was not drunk. Then he looked again. It was still there: Mars for the Martians.

It is not, contrary to most people's ideas, lonely being an astronomer. You may be sitting up at night, all by yourself, but once you look through your telescope, you are surrounded by millions of worlds, jostled by stars, hurtling along a crowded celestial motorway. There is so much going on out there that you don't feel lonely.

But you don't expect to see Mars for the Martians written in the heavens, either.

There was something else, too. Since he had started watching it, this miraculous message had moved faster than any heavenly body he had ever come across. Unless, of course, it was much closer than he realized. Yes, that was it; being so close made it look as if it were moving fast . . . He stiffened. Now there was another message in the sky: Krypton United for the Galactic Cup!

'I don't believe it,' said Professor Greenloft.
'Have you told anyone else?' asked Sir Dudley Wishbone, the most famous living ex-astronomer.

'I came straight to you,' said Professor Greenloft. 'I thought I might have contracted Kirschner's madness.' Kirschner was a Belgian astronomer who had first identified the condition which attacks all astronomers sooner or later; the belief that the stars form logical patterns. In Kirschner's case he thought he had found stars forming his mother's likeness in the Milky Way. Convinced that he had gone mad through too much star-watching, he shot himself. Later, tragically, they found the unmistakable portrait of a bad-tempered-looking Belgian lady with a lace head-dress in the sky and named it Old Mrs Kirschner in his honour.

'You don't look mad to me,' said Sir Dudley. 'Let's have a look at these heavenly graffiti of yours.'

Greenloft already had the telescope set up. The Martian graffiti was still there and so was the Krypton United one, but there were now lots more, like: Venusians Do it Standing on Their Left Legs, and Alpha Centauri Bovver Boys Were Here, and Martian Time-share Is a Racket, and A Vote for President Grig of Glunt Is a Vote for the Future.

'You aren't imagining things,' said Sir Dudley. 'There really are graffiti in space.'

'Not quite in space,' said Greenloft. 'I have computed that they occur at the very edge of our atmosphere, by the so-called ozone layer. My theory is that it's all connected with the greenhouse effect, and our use of aerosols. As we all know by now, the chemicals used in aerosols gather on the edge of the atmosphere. We also know that graffiti are made by aerosol sprays. Is is not possible in some strange way that the aerosol spray is drifting to the edge of space and *reforming there in the shape of galactic graffiti?*'

There was a silence. Sir Dudley looked through the telescope again at the teeming heavens. Two new graffiti had appeared on the edge of space. One said: God Does Not Exist. The other said: Oh Yes, I Do.

'No, Greenloft,' said the elderly ex-astronomer. 'It is a good theory but it is not a true theory. I believe the truth is much more disturbing and more interesting than that.'

The Celestial Greenhouse Part Two

Today we conclude our thrilling new science fiction serial, 'The Graffiti Effect'. Professor Greenloft, the greatest living astronomer, has discovered graffiti in the ozone layer, caused perhaps by aerosol deposits. Sir Dudley Wishbone, greatest living ex-astronomer, thinks there is a more uncanny explanation.

'I don't know about you,' said Sir Dudley, 'but I've never ever seen anyone writing graffiti.'

'Nor I,' said Greenloft.

'Yet despite having no evidence, you believe that graffiti are written by real people?'

'Yes,' said Greenloft.

'The same should apply to the graffiti you have spotted in the skies. I think we can assume that your celestial messages, which seem to appear from nowhere, are written by a verifiable agency.'

'What, like an advertising or PR agency?' said Greenloft, puzzled.

'Although that is rather a stupid remark, it may be nearer to the truth than you think,' said Sir Dudley. 'Now, you referred earlier to the greenhouse effect. People have talked a lot about this. It has driven them to study aerosol chemicals, and the ozone layer, and ultraviolet light, and many other things. But there is one thing they have forgotten to study.'

'That being?'

'Greenhouses.'

Professor Greenloft nodded sagely, as one does when one is not sure if one's companion is being very intelligent or going round the twist.

'Since I abandoned full-time astronomy,' said Sir Dudley, 'I have been studying greenhouses, to see what we can learn about the universe. People always forget that there are many more greenhouse effects than just trapping heat inside glass.'

'Such as?'

'Such as the tendency to have seed packets lying around, well past their sell-by date. Such as the proliferation of rusty, clapped-out tools. Such as a small ant trail across the floor. Such as cracked and abandoned little pots. Such as hand-written labels which have survived the plants they were meant to be describing. Such . . .'

'Hold on, hold on!' cried Greenloft. 'This is all true enough, but what on earth can it tell us about the world we live in?'

'More than you might think. Have you ever noticed that the world is also filling up with rusty, old, clapped-out equipment?'

'Well, I suppose so, but . . .'

'Have you ever realized just how full the world is of ancient, written or carved inscriptions in languages we cannot understand?'

'You mean – like old flower labels and tags?'

'Precisely. The world we live in is just like a greenhouse; it's just that nobody has ever spelt out the similarities before.'

'That's rather far-fetched, surely. What about the abandoned flower pots?'

'It is my belief that if you dug down into Silbury Hill, the Pyramids and many other strangely conical structures, you would find an enormous flower pot concealed therein beneath the compost of ages.'

'What is the equivalent of seed packets past their sell-by dates?'

'Oh, extinct and near-extinct species.'

'And the ants on the greenhouse floor?'

Sir Dudley leant forward and tapped Greenloft on the shoulder.

'Us, dear boy, us. Man is the ant on the floor of the solar greenhouse. We think the greenhouse is for our benefit but it is not. Somebody has created this greenhouse we call the earth, and its atmosphere, to grow something, but it is not us.'

'None of which explains the graffiti.'

'And I suspect they are no longer growing it, whatever it was,' continued Sir Dudley as if he had not heard, 'because the most striking greenhouse effect of all is to be abandoned. I would wager that fully half the greenhouses you see in gardens are disused; overgrown; returning to nature; rusty and wild; falling down. And I think the earth is being allowed to go to rack and ruin by the greenhouse owner.'

He lapsed into silence. Greenloft did not known whether to say anything.

'And when things get disused and dirty,' he said suddenly, 'people start writing graffiti on the outside. You thought the graffiti were coming from our side. I think not. Someone or some people are writing with their fingers on the outside of our atmosphere. And the next step, I fear, will be demolition.'

In the ensuing silence. Professor Greenloft glanced through his telescope at the graffiti area. There was a new, even more chilling graffiti, recently written. It said: 'Dirty'.

Gardeners' Put-down Time

CULTIVATE *your garden, said Voltaire. It was the most detailed gardening advice he ever gave. Probably it was the only thing he knew about gardening. A fat lot of good he would have been on Gardeners' Question Time. Luckily, we have today a far greater gardening expert than Voltaire to answer your gardening queries: Ted Glurk.*

This has been the mildest winter I can remember since records began (which was of course in 1870 with Thomas Edison), and many springtime flowers have made an appearance in my garden long before they were due. The blossom is dancing on every tree, the birds are piping a joyous song and the careless hum of full many a summer insect can be heard o'er the early-verdant lawn. SK of Bristol

Ted Glurk writes: All right, we get the idea. No need to go over the top. What's your question?

Is there anything I can do to protect these early visitors when a fiercely cold spell comes, as come it surely will? S K of Bristol

Ted Glurk writes: No.

Oh, come on, there must be something. S K of Bristol

Ted Glurk writes: Like what?

Well, I don't see why I couldn't bring the garden indoors. I have a large house, most of it disused, and it shouldn't take more than a day or two to get the bulk of the shallower blooms dug up and brought in on stretchers. Again, it should be possible to roof over the garden with a cheap flexiglass dome, or perhaps an expensive kind of clingfilm. Or maybe I could even erect vast warm air blowers in my hedgerows which would keep the atmosphere over my lawn springlike until the real spring arrived. S K again

Ted Glurk writes: You're welcome to try. Next please.

I often travel on business from the Midlands, where I live, to London, and there I find that Londoners can still scarcely believe that we suffered no damage from the hurricane in October 1987. While discussing the subject I try to think of a way of expressing enormous sympathy with their plight while at the same time hinting at a lingering satisfaction that London and the South-east were not entirely unscathed. Can you suggest any subtle phraseology? G V of Walsall

Ted Glurk writes: No. Can you?

Well, how about: 'Serves you right, you smug southern bastards'? G V of Walsall

Ted Glurk: You're welcome to try. Next please.

The forecasters have been forecasting storms, hurricanes and God knows what for the last three months, but it has been the most wonderfully warm winter I can remember. Can you explain this discrepancy? F C of Hull

Ted Glurk writes: No. Can you?

Well, I expect that as a result of not wanting to be caught out by another hurricane, they've been given orders to forecast the worst possible weather at any time. That's my theory, anyway. F C of Hull

Ted Glurk: And you're welcome to it. Another question.

Yes. How come, if you're a gardening expert, you don't know any of the answers to these questions? And why can't you at least pretend to be pleasant? N S of Tyneside

Ted Glurk: That's easy. I've noticed that all gardening experts on radio and TV are indistinguishable. That's because they're all boring, kindly, good-hearted old buffers. And people are getting sick of it. So I decided that the only way to break into the game was to be the first grumpy, no-nonsense, leave-me-alone gardening expert. The Basil Fawlty of the herbaceous border. The Enoch Powell of the potting shed.

Thank you. That's an interesting idea. Can I appear on your TV show when you get one? N S of Tyneside.

Ted Glurk: No, you can't. Get lost. Next please.

I have a small, bare, north-facing wall which needs something on it. Can you suggest what I should do with it? J D of Bath

Ted Glurk: Look, this is small-time stuff. Hasn't anyone out there got big-time problems?

Yes. I own a large football stadium which is only used for half the year. Can you suggest anything more profitable for summer sowing than merely replacement grass? F B of Chelsea

Ted Glurk writes: Now you're talking! For a summer crop in football stadiums, I highly recommend the cannabis plant, which not only grows quickly and looks nice, but also makes a whole lot more money than football. I have a few plants in my own nursery, if you're interested. Pop around any evening for a quick look. Next please.

Hello. I am Chief Superintendent Wilkins, and I am arresting you on a charge of growing certain substances. It is my duty to tell you that anything you might say . . .

Ted Glurk writes: OK, OK, it's a fair cop. I'm coming.

Ted Glurk will be back soon to answer more of your questions. There again, perhaps he won't. Perhaps it will be someone else. Maybe even Voltaire. Who knows? It's a funny old game, gardening.

Thatcher and God: a Progress Report

MRS THATCHER has been having an informal series of talks with God. That much is clear. It is also clear that the talks took place at Mrs Thatcher's prompting. Sources say that it was difficult for God to make time to come to 10 Downing Street, but that Mrs Thatcher insisted that the talks were vital.

Further than that, very little is known about what went on. The contents of the talks are, of course, highly secret and private, but it is understood that Mrs Thatcher let her displeasure at God's current progress be known. As society becomes more prosperous (for which Mrs Thatcher's government can take the credit), the standard of private morality is going down, and this could only be laid at God's door. What Mrs Thatcher wanted to know was, what was God going to do about it?

God was about to answer, when Mrs Thatcher proceeded to make some suggestions. The nature of these is, of course, completely confidential, but it is understood Mrs Thatcher made the following proposals to God.

1. That God should ensure that if mankind was made in God's image, it should be better made in future, as standards of people-manufacture to her seemed very shoddy at the moment, with especially low levels of enterprise, honesty and industriousness-control.

2. That God should soften the hearts of the heads of state in the European Community, so that they should understand the appalling error of their ways over agriculture.

3. That, for heaven's sake, God should generally buck his ideas up, and buck up the ideas of the Archbishop of Canterbury in particular.

What God said in reply to these three suggestions is not, as might be expected, on record, as the entire talks were confidential, but I am given to understand that God's answers were not entirely satisfactory to Mrs Thatcher. She then went on to review God's past performance, pointing out his inability to control climate, population and disease at various points of history, and wonder if He had really learnt from experience.

At this point God is believed to have pleaded an urgent engagement (some say a progress review with Mr Pat Robertson, others an invitation to Australia's Bicentennial) and the talks ended. Shortly afterwards, a miracle took place; a flash of lightning was seen, there was a roll of thunder, and the radiant form of Mrs Thatcher's private archangel, Bernard, appeared. The throng of journalists did marvel at this sight, and then asked him what had taken place at the talks.

The archangel Bernard made it clear that the talks were absolutely private and secret, and that Mrs Thatcher respected God's privacy as a statesman of equal standing. However, if anyone had any questions, he was happy to answer them off the record. What then transpired is, of course, secret but the following exchanges took place:

'How did Mrs Thatcher address God?'

'She generally called him 'Sir Robin'.'

'How did God seem?'

'Nervous, ill-at-ease, not sure how to handle the situation.'

'In what way?'

'He did not seem used to not being in full charge of the flow of discourse.'

'Does that mean being unable to get a word in edgeways?'

'Yes. Presumably He did not understand fully that He was there to listen to what Mrs Thatcher had to say, not the other way round.'

'Are any more meetings planned?'

'She has requested God to be present at further talks so that she can review His progress in the light of her suggestions. One expects He will be there.'

What God thinks of the talks is, of course, not known, as the whole series of exchanges were totally informal and private. It is, however, understood that God regularly appears to the Archbishop of Canterbury in a dream to urge him to ordain women and to design a new uniform for Church of England clergy. On His most recent appearance I understand that He seemed very upset. The Archbishop tells friends that God was quite shaken, and muttered to himself a lot about patience and long-suffering.

God is supposed to have told the Archbishop that she was after His guts. When the Archbishop suggested that God might have directed the Prime Minister's attention to the beam in her government's eye, God is said to have grown heated and replied: 'Do you think I didn't try?'

'I have never seen Him so angry,' the Archbishop is reported as saying. This does not bode well for the next series of talks at Number 10, which will, of course, be totally confidential; full details will be printed in this space.

Some People Do, and
Some People Don't

THERE are two different kinds of people. There are those who lay the table for breakfast the night before, and those who lay the table as they are actually eating breakfast.

There are people who fasten their seat belts as soon as they get into the driver's seat, and those who wait until they are driving at 30 mph and confident that the car is actually going to make it before they endanger everyone else's lives by struggling into their belts with one hand while changing gear with the other.

There are people who like pop music and people who think that Peter Gabriel is a character in *The Archers*.

There are those who write postcards on the first day of the holiday and those who write them on the last.

There are people who smile when having their pictures taken in a passport photo booth (and come out looking like lunatics) and those who prefer a thoughtful expression (the murderers).

There are people who, when asked what they would like to drink, mistakenly think that it is helpful to say: 'Oh, I don't mind – anything will do', and those who avoid being throttled by actually naming something.

There are those who will gladly choose a new and interesting-sounding dish on a menu, and those who, afraid of anything unfamiliar, will persuade someone else at the table to choose it, so that they can have a taste.

There are people who carry photographs of their family about with them, and people who are travelling to get away from them.

There are men who, if asked by the police to describe what their wife was wearing that morning, would be able to specify every garment, and those who could not even remember the colour of her eyes.

There are people who always feel sorry for buskers and put something into their hat and there are those who look into the hat and think: 'By gum, I wish I was making that sort of money'.

There are those people who react to a breakage by thinking: 'I must mend that', and those who think: 'I must get a new one'.

There are those who think that an undercooked boiled egg, with a wobbly transparent white, is the most disgusting thing in the world and there are those who think that that title is a walkover for overcooked scrambled egg.

There are letter-writers who use a fresh sheet for each new side, but there are also letter-writers who turn over their first sheet and start their second side on the back of the first, *and* number it 2, *and* then go on writing because they think it looks wrong to sign off at the top of a page.

There are those who are miserably obsessed with the idea that they might have bad breath, but don't, and there are those who have no idea that they might have, and do.

There are people who haven't looked at their own signature for years, and people who are uneasily aware that they do it somewhat differently each time, no matter how hard they try to do it without thinking.

There are people who leave a spare house key outside under the mat (in the flower pot, behind the drainpipe, under the garden gnome, etc) and there are those who have been burgled already.

There are some who, when a watch starts going wrong, learn to adjust quite adequately by adding five minutes to the time shown or subtracting eight and a half minutes per day, etc, and there are others who go and get the thing mended.

There are those who watch television programmes they have recorded on video but don't keep them, and those who keep them but don't watch them.

There are people who can take out staples with their finger-nails and those who can't.

There are those who think that Britain is a class-ridden society, and those who think it doesn't matter either way as long as you know your place in the set-up.

There are some who can remove splinters from their own bodies without thinking and some who have to get an ambulance or half a dozen relatives to do it for them; the same goes for removing sticky plaster and bits of grit from the eye.

There are those who can deal efficiently with the apparently invisible and unlocatable end of a roll of Sellotape, and those who are reduced to trembling wrecks by the whole business.

There are those who, when they get to the bottom of a page in a magazine which reads 'Continued on page 136', turn to page 136 to continue, and those who angrily turn to some other article.

(*Continued on page 136*)

Another Fine Casserole You've Got Me in

CHARACTERS in English thrillers, says a critic, never seem to bother much about literature or good cooking. Well, that's easily rectified by today's complete thriller.

The burglars had been very careful. They had not taken anything. They had just contented themselves with opening the kitchen window and cooking a rabbit casserole, with mushrooms and red wine. I tried it. It was delicious. Then I sent for the police.

'Came in through the kitchen window, eh?' said Constable Mitcham. 'Then cooked a rabbit casserole? Well, I don't think we can really call them burglars at all, as they didn't take anything.'

'They took my rabbit from the fridge,' I said indignantly. 'That's theft. Not to mention my red wine.'

'And mushrooms,' mused the constable. 'They took your mushrooms as well.'

'Not true,' I conceded. 'There were no mushrooms on the premises. They must have brought those with them.'

There was a short silence as Constable Mitcham wrote laboriously in his notebook. (Why is it that policemen always write laboriously? Why does none of them ever write fluently, with an instinctive grasp of character interplay, as our leading novelists always do?) I looked over his shoulder as he wrote . . .

'I shuddered as I glanced into the rabbit casserole,' I read. 'There, nearly hidden in the middle of the rich gallimaufry of redolent flesh, rendered fungi and rechauffé Fleurie, lay the unmistakable outline of a human hand! It looked well cooked. What horrible crime had led to this heartless ragout?'

Two things were immediately obvious to me. One was that I had been quite wrong about the constable's literary abilities and I owed him an apology.

'I'd like to apologize for thinking you wrote laboriously, officer.'

'That's all right, sir. At least you didn't think that I licked the end of my pencil before continuing my painfully slow scratching in my notebook. What about the human hand, then, sir?'

That was the other thing. Together we stared into the meaty recesses of the rabbit stew, and there, sure enough, was the unmistakable outline of a human hand. It was yellowish in hue, and one of the fingers was bent at an impossible angle.

'We have two crimes here,' said the constable. 'The theft of some mushrooms, and the murder of an unknown person. You, by your own admission, took the mushrooms. It seems logical to assume that you are also guilty of the murder.'

'It is not in the least logical.'

'No,' he admitted, 'but it saves a lot of time.'

He started writing in his notebook again and again I looked over his shoulder.

'Brian had now come to that stage in life where all men think of having one last fling,' I read, 'and start treating their wives better to compensate for it. Brian's wife, who knew everything that was going through his mind, was flattered by the attention, but secretly hoped he would have his little fling and get it over with . . .'

'What on earth is all that about?' I exclaimed.

'You mustn't believe that everything policemen write in their books is evidence,' he said. 'I myself am writing a novel during working hours. Other officers I know prefer poetry or military history. It's very personal.'

At that moment my wife arrived back home. She raised her eyebrows at the sight of the policeman.

'You didn't tell me you were bringing a friend home, George,' she said.

'No,' I said,' actually . . .'

'What can you tell me about this rabbit casserole, madam?' interrupted the policeman.

'The casserole?' said my wife. 'Well, you soften some onions in butter, then you put in the bacon . . .'

'Do you mean to say that you cooked this?'

'Who else? Do you think that burglars burst in and cooked it?'

As the policeman and I looked at each other, she turned to the sink and found the pile of washing-up I had meant to do before she got back.

'George, you are hopeless. And where have you put the other washing-up glove?'

Before I could say anything, Constable Mitcham suddenly leant forward and pulled the yellow hand out of the rabbit stew. It was a washing-up glove.

'I think that clears up everything,' said Mitcham, licking his pencil and picking up his notebook. 'Except for the rabbit casserole recipe. It is my duty to warn you that anything you say will be taken down and given to a colleague who is compiling a cookery book.'

Oh, Fred, Our Help in Ages Past

SEVERAL years ago I stayed the night at the excellent George Hotel at Stamford in Lincolnshire. While I was browsing my way through breakfast, I became aware of a conversation at a nearby table between a young American businessman and a rather older English counterpart. At first I made no attempt to listen. Business conversations always put me to sleep, and I had only just woken up.

But I changed my mind when I realized that there was some deep emotional undertow in their exchanges. The Englishman, who looked shiny and nervous, was trying to justify his activities on behalf of the firm. The recently arrived American was looking sympathetic, but this was in direct contrast to his words which were highly critical of what the Englishman was defending. I realized after a few minutes that in all probability the Englishman was about to be given the sack, and that the American had come over from New York to do it.

I had never eavesdropped on someone being given the heave-ho before, and I was careful to make a note of the technique. It was devilishly clever. The American was hiding behind the skirts of someone called Fred, who was back in New York, and using Fred to deflect every counter-blow.

'We have honestly made the fastest possible progress in introducing new techniques,' the Englishman would say.

'Gee, Bill, I really believe that,' the American would answer. 'I only wish I could get Fred to see it that way.'

Or again: 'So that's the programme we envisage for the next three years.'

'And a good little programme it is too, Bill. Unfortunately, it's not at all the one that Fred had in mind.'

It was a refinement of the police technique which involves questioning by one nice and one nasty policeman, only in this case the nasty policeman wasn't even there; his part was played *in absentia* by the nice policeman. Somewhere in New York, there was a senior executive called Fred in whose name anything could be said or done.

'Look, I think I ought to talk to Fred direct,' said the desperate Englishman at one point. 'I'll phone him or even fly to New York and talk to him.'

'I don't think Fred would appreciate that,' said the young man quietly. 'That sort of approach tends to upset Fred. I think that could be very unwise on your part. After all, I am here to act for Fred, and that's what he wants me to do.'

The reason I have remembered this chilling little conversation so long is that I keep being reminded of it whenever the part of Fred is played by God. The way God is invoked by Christians, or Allah by Muslims, is remarkably similar. Many godly people are humble and undeserving, as they readily remind you, but God is rather different; God takes a very dim view indeed of what you are up to. Take their word for it.

The Fred technique is seen in quite pure form in the words and actions of the Rev Ian Paisley, who chucklingly invokes a wrathful Fred as well as an ever-open hell where Fred will send wicked people.

But the purest Fred technique I ever saw was that used by my lovely but merciless cleaning lady in London. She hailed from St Kitts in the West Indies, where they seemed to specialize in a fairly threatening form of Freddism.

'See you on Tuesday,' I would cry merrily on Thursday.

'If life lasts,' she would rejoin gaily.

'I'm sure it will,' I would sometimes rejoin, unwisely.

'How can you know? Who gives you the right to be sure about life? Only God can give us life, and He may take it away any moment! Are you ready to face Him . . .?'

It was sometimes hard work saying goodbye to her, but it helped if I remembered that it was really Fred she was invoking. Indeed, it has helped me a lot since. Whenever I hear God called upon as a reason to ban a film, invade Nicaragua or stop women being priests, it usually turns out be Fred, not God, who is involved. Fred is not always called God. He is sometimes called Marx, sometimes Brecht, sometimes Mao. Sometimes Fred changes slightly to Freud. But he is always recognizable as that shady, frightening, unknowable figure whose word is law and who cannot be contacted directly.

'Fred would be very upset if you got in touch with him. I am here to act for Fred and that is what he wants me to do.' It is the voice of the lawyer, the psychiatrist, the Christian, the secret policeman and the bureaucrat through the ages. Fred moves in a mysterious way. I have my doubts about the existence of God, but I am a fervent believer in Fred.

And in the Beginning Was Soap

ITV wants to get rid of the early Sunday evening religious broadcast, the so-called God slot. The IBA wants to keep it, for fear it might be replaced by a soap opera or similar. So I have been working feverishly on a solution which will satisfy both sides, and here it is – a soap opera which is actually based on the Bible. To give you some idea, here's an extract from an early episode.

Story so far. God has created the world and Adam has opened the first gardening centre. As time goes by things get out of hand on Earth; God is sorry he let Man run the show and has decided to drown every human except Noah and his family, thus cutting the cast to low-budget proportions.

Mrs Noah is in the kitchen, cutting sandwiches for Noah before he goes out to resume work on the Ark.

Mrs Noah: God called while you were out, dear.

Noah: Did he leave a message?

Mrs Noah: He wanted to know how the Ark was getting on, and if you were using the best quality gopher wood.

Noah: Course I'm using the best possible wood!

Mrs Noah: Says that if you use duff gopher wood, and the Ark sinks, and we drown, that's it. He's not going to make any more people.

Noah: God's trouble is, He can't delegate properly. Always coming round to check up.

Mrs Noah: Do you want honey and locust on brown?

Noah: Yes, please.

Mrs Noah: Another thing. He said, watch out for Shem and Ham's wife. They're having a bit of an affair, and he won't stand for any Ark-board romances. Tell them to cut it out, He says.

Noah: Shem and Ham's wife? I don't believe it! How does He know?

Mrs Noah: He knows everything.

Noah: Then why does He come snooping round to see how the Ark is getting on if He already knows?

Mrs Noah: Because it's a way of getting you to get a move on, stupid.

Noah: Yes, but . . . Blimey, here comes my father. Now, remember, God says we can't take him on the Ark, so don't tell him anything. *Exit Noah, smartish.*

Mrs Noah: For God's sake, don't leave me alone with the old . . . *Enter Lamech, Noah's Dad, getting on a bit now at 777 years old, but good for his age.*

Lamech: Hello. Where's Noah?

Mrs Noah: Hello, Grandad. He's out working on his Ark. Look, I've got piles of things to do . . .

Lamech: Has he said anything about the maiden voyage yet? His mother and I can't understand why we haven't been invited.

Mrs Noah: This first trip is just a test to see if the Ark works, and he doesn't want to risk you and Mum on board.

Lamech: But there's plenty of room for us. It's got about 400 cabins. We wouldn't get in the way.

Mrs Noah: Dad! The answer's No!

Lamech: He's drifting apart from me, Noah is. All this money and big ideas has gone to his head. Just because he's 500 years old, he thinks he knows everything. He's changed since he got married.

Mrs Noah: I suppose you blame me.

Lamech: No, love, I don't. I've always liked you. In fact, I've liked you more than you probably realize. You've got a lovely body for a 470-year-old, and if I were fifty years younger . . . *Lamech clumsily puts an arm round her waist.*

Mrs Noah: You dirty old . . .! You just wait till Noah hears about this!

Lamech: I wouldn't tell my son anything, love. Or I might have to tell him about you and the gopher wood man.

Mrs Noah: Gopher wood . . .? Just how much do you know? *Lamech is about to tell her when he has a heart attack and keels over backwards.*

Enter Ham.

Ham: Hello, Mum, seen Mrs Shem anywhere? Oh my God, what's wrong with Grandad?

Enter Shem in a towering rage.

Shem: Ham, you bastard, I've just found out about you and my wife. If you think I'm letting you come on the Ark to save your sordid little life, then you've got another think . . .?

Enter Noah, just as Shem is about to lay out Ham, and Lamech his father is starting to regain consciousness on the new Canaanite floor tiling.

Noah: I forgot to take my lunch box. What on earth . . .? *There is thunderous knocking off stage and a servant girl rushes in.*

Servant: Please, Noah, sir, God is at the door and He wants to know if you'll be ready for rain at the weekend.

Noah opens his mouth, but we don't hear what he says, because the theme music for 'The Chosen' comes up, for the end of the episode. Next week: An elephant steps on Lamech and we learn something startling about Noah and Mrs Japheth.

Murder on the InterCity Express

TODAY, a complete murder mystery story! See if you can spot who the killer is. All the clues are somewhere in the story . . .

The midnight express roared through the night. Adrian sat and dozed slightly. England lay asleep all around him as he hurtled from Paddington towards his destination.

Actually, England lay asleep inside the train as well – in the next seat along from him a businessman lay sprawled across the table, snoring. He was out for the count, exhausted and faded. If the cellular phone in front of him on the table rang, he didn't suppose he would even hear it.

Much to Adrian's pleasure, the phone rang at that very moment. Would it go unanswered? The phone stopped ringing; there was a series of clicks and whispers; a loud beep was heard; all of which meant that the call had been dealt with by a telephone answering machine.

Adrian's observations were cut short by the arrival of a British Rail steward who leant over him and said softly: 'Do you wish to play, sir?'

'Play what?' said Adrian, puzzled.

'Play the tables, sir. Roulette, blackjack, baccarat, anything you like. The casino coach is just two along from here, next to the buffet.'

Adrian, like many people, was unaware of the enormous strides British Rail has made in trying to keep customers happy. Mobile casinos, Nightrider disco coaches, aisle street theatre – you can find everything these days.

After two hours at the tables, Adrian had won £5,000, but, after tipping the croupier, buying several rounds of drinks and paying for a first-class ticket (he had only come equipped with a cheap saver) he found himself slightly out of pocket. Still, he had enjoyed himself and that was the main thing, he thought, as he returned to his seat. There was someone sitting in it.

'That's my seat,' said Adrian.

The man smiled but did not get up. Instead he produced a badge and showed it to Adrian. It read: British Rail Police.

'I wonder if you can tell me anything about the gentleman in the seat behind us.'

He was still there, fast asleep, tumbled over the table, vibrating with the train.

'He's been asleep since the train started, as far as I know. I presume he has spent all day working on marketing strategy for a brand of poisonous fizzy orange drink and is now dog tired.'

'Nevertheless, sir, I'd be grateful if you would go and wake him up. Ask him what station he's getting out at, something like that.'

Adrian shook him, softly first, then roughly. The man fell sideways. He was dead.

'You see,' said the policeman, 'you were, as far as I can make out, the only other person here at the time of his death. You might be able to tell me something.'

'Nothing at all,' said Adrian. 'Oh, except that his phone rang once.'

'Did you hear him speaking?'

'He didn't wake up. The message was recorded on his device, though.'

'Was it, now? Well, perhaps we'd better go and listen to it.'

With some difficulty they disentangled the dead man from his telecommunications apparatus. They found the tape. They wound it back. They played it. This is what it said:

'Robert – this is a message of vital importance. Mackinlay-Keys is somewhere on the train. He's after you. He'll kill you if he gets the chance. So for God's sake look out! Give me a ring back any time, no matter how late it is.'

'I'm certainly glad you knew about the message, sir,' said the policeman. 'It's going to be a vital clue. May I have your name for reference?'

'My name is Adrian Mackinlay-Keys,' said Adrian with some difficulty, 'and I swear to you, officer, that I have never seen this man before in my life. Most of the time I have been in the casino coach. The croupier will swear to that.'

'Casino coach? That's a new one on me, sir. Would you care to show me this mobile gambling den?'

Adrian took him along to show him the tables. They were not there. The coach had totally vanished, as if it had never been. Adrian suddenly found himself caught in a quite terrifying nightmare from which he could see no exit.

Well, did you solve the mystery? The answer, of course, is that Adrian was on a British Rail Murder Weekend, one of the very popular entertainments now being organized to fill off-peak services, and all the people involved were actors. If you'd like to know more about British Rail outings, just write to their Showbiz section today.

The Beaufort Rain Scale

IT HAS always surprised me that Beaufort worked out his scale for wind, not for rain. Rain, surely, has always been more important to the British and more talked about by us than any other bit of weather. Wet and damp are what we fear most, far more than draughts and breezes, yet nobody as far as I know has had shot at a Beaufort Rain Scale. Well, here goes then:

FORCE 0. Complete dryness. Absence of rain from the air. The gap between two periods of wet. Associated phrase: 'I think it looks like rain.'

FORCE 1. Presence of wet in the air, hovering rather than falling. Scotch mist. You can feel damp on your face but if you supinate your hand, nothing lands on it. Associated phrase: 'I think it's trying to rain.'

FORCE 2. Individual drops of rain falling, but quite separate as if they are all freelance raindrops and not part of the same corporate effort. If switched on now, windscreen wipers make an awful screeching noise. Spectacle wearers begin to grumble. Newspaper being read outside begins to speckle. Associated phrase: 'It's spitting.'

FORCE 3. Raindrops falling together now, but still invisibly, like the spray which drifts off a fountain with the wind behind. Known as 'fine rain'. Ignored by all sportsmen except Test cricketers, who dash for cover. Spectacle wearers walk into oncoming traffic. Windscreen wipers, when switched on, make windscreen totally opaque. If being read outside, newspaper gets rising damp. Associated phrases: 'Is it worth putting the umbrella up?' 'Another fine rain you've got us into'.

FORCE 4. Visible light shower. Hair starts to congeal round ears. First rainwear appears. People start to remember washing left out. Ignored by all sportsmen except Wimbledon players, who sprint for cover. Newspaper being read outside starts to tear slightly. Associated phrases: 'It's starting to come down now', 'It won't last', 'It's settled in for the day now'.

FORCE 5. Drizzle. Shapes beginning to be visible in rain for first time, usually drifting from right to left. Windscreen wipers too slow at low speed, too fast at fast speed. Shower-proof rainwear turns out to be shower-proof all right, but not drizzle-proof. First damp feeling inside either shoes or neckline. Butterflies take evasive action and begin to fly straight. Newspaper being read in the open starts turning to pulp.

Associated phrases: 'It's really chucking it down now', 'It's raining cats and dogs', 'Nice for the farmers'.

FORCE 6. Downpour. You can see raindrops bouncing on impact, like charter planes landing. Leaves and petals recoil when hit. Anything built of concrete starts to look nasty. Eyebrows become waterlogged. Horse racing called off. Wet feeling rises above ankles and starts for knees. Butterflies fly backwards. Newspaper being read in open divides in two. Gardeners watering the flowers start thinking about packing it in. Associated phrases: 'It's coming down in stair rods', 'It's bucketing down'.

FORCE 7. Squally, gusty rain. As Force 6, but with added wind. Water starts being forced up your nostrils. Maniacs leave home and head for motorway in their cars. Butterflies start walking. Household cats and dogs become unpleasant to handle. Cheaper clothes start coming to bits. Associated phrases: 'It's pissing down now', 'There's some madman out in the garden trying to read a newspaper'.

FORCE 8. Torrential. The whole outside world has been turned into an *en suite* douche. It starts raining inside umbrellas. Windscreen wipers become useless. The ground looks as if it is steaming. Butterflies drown. Your garments start merging into each other and becoming indistinguishable. Man reading newspaper in the open starts disintegrating. All team games called off except football, rugby and water polo. Associated phrase: 'Jesus, will you look at that coming down?'

FORCE 9. Cloudburst. Rain so fierce that it can only be maintained for a minute or two. Drops so large that they hurt if they hit you. Water gets into pockets and forms rock pools. Windscreen wipers are torn off cars. Too wet for water-skiing. Instantaneous rivers form on roads, and man reading a newspaper floats past. Rain runs UP windows.

FORCE 10. Hurricane. Not known in this country – the symptoms are too violent and extreme (cars floating, newspaper readers lost at sea, people drowned by inhaling rain, etc). So if hurricane conditions do appear to pertain, look for some other explanation. Associated phrases: 'Oh my God, the water tank has burst – it's coming through the kitchen ceiling!', 'I think the man upstairs has fallen asleep in his bath', etc.

Baby's First Year: Unofficial

BEING a father again has given me lots of wonderful material which I refuse to use on the grounds that it would embarrass my son when he grows up. But I think I should make an exception to this if at any time I discover a radical change we should make to the way we bring up children. Today is one of those occasions.

Specifically, I would like to change the format of those albums called *Baby's First Year* or *Baby's Little Book* which are filled in and then forgotten for ever. These books always contain boxes labelled 'My weight at one month was . . .', 'My first tooth arrived on the . . .' and other such milestones.

Unfortunately, it is not the milestones we want to remember, it is the significant happenings between the milestones, those events which are not even mentioned by *Our Infant's First Twelve Months*. So I propose that the following entries should immediately replace the current ones in all such books.

*The name I have been given is . . .

*Shortened to . . .

*My grandparents, not liking either of these names at all, prefer to call me . . .

*My parents, not liking the name used by my grandparents, have taken to calling them a pair of interfering old . . .

*What I actually tend to be called most of the time is Chubby Legs/Sunshine/Beautiful.

*When I am called Chubby Legs, or Sunshine, or Beautiful, I feel like throwing up. The first day on which I actually threw up was . . .

*The day on which a grown-up first called me Chubby Legs and made me throw up and then said: 'Poor little thing, he has been a little icky, I wonder why on earth' was . . .

*The amount of bibs I have been bought is . . .

*The amount of bibs that can actually be found at any one time in the house is . . .

*The weight of my bib before meals is . . .

*The weight of my bib after meals is . . .

*If my bib were boiled in a saucepan after several meals, it would make a soup nutritious enough to feed . . . people.

*The day I realized that we babies wore bibs when we were fed but the person feeding you didn't wear a bib was . . .

*The day I realized you could take advantage of this by blowing food

106

over them or clutching their clothes fondly was . . .

*The day my parents started wearing bibs was . . .

*The amount of time it took me to invent an entirely new language using only the letters B and G and M, and making words like 'mamamamam' and 'babababab', was . . . days.

*The amount of time it took me to teach this language to my parents and get them speaking it was . . . days.

*The day on which I realized my parents could speak the language but not understand it – that, for instance, they had no idea 'mamamamam' means 'Can I have a chew of the evening paper when you've finished with it?' or that 'bubububub' is short for 'Either that rhubarb yoghurt goes or I do' – was . . .

*The day I gave up speaking this language but my parents went on speaking it was . . .

*Apart from beautiful, the word most often used by my parents to describe me is dirty/mucky/messy.

*The day I found out that they were using these words as euphemisms for perfectly ordinary bowel functions was . . .

*The day I work out why one of my parents should bother to use euphemisms when he and I are the only ones in the room and he isn't even talking to me will be . . .

*It took me . . . months to realize that you did not have to undo a shoe to get it off.

*Using only my feet, I can now get off either shoe in . . . seconds flat.

*The thing that annoys my parents most is: my crying inexplicably/my refusing a meal they have cooked specially for me/my waking up early after they have had a late night/them finding only one shoe.

*The thing that annoys me most is: my parents shouting inexplicably/my failing to get a repeat of a favourite meal/my being woken up at night by my parents wanting to show me off to some visitors/losing only one shoe.

*My parents have given me some really wonderful naturally crafted toys, which I ignore completely in favour of: a wooden kitchen spoon/anything plastic/the half-finished bottles of white wine in the door of the fridge/the inside of my parents' ears.

*Being taken for a piggy-back is fun because you can: see all the very interesting and educational things going on around you/gradually and patiently increase the small bald patch on your father's head.

All Quiet on the Glorious Twelfth

'QUIET out there,' said McAllister. 'Too damned quiet for my liking,' said Duncan Wood.

Together they stared out into the gathering gloom. From their positions they could just make out the line of the woodland across the two or three hundred yards of moorland which separated them from it. They had built rudimentary defences of wood, and had a couple of rifles between them, but any determined rush would certainly sweep them away. They could not see anything moving in the woods at all, but they knew the woods were full of them.

'How many do you suppose there are?' 'Four or five thousand.' 'What do you think they are up to?'

'Hard to say. You never know what the grouse are thinking. People always say they're a stupid bird, but in my experience they learn fast if given the chance. The old Earl of Inverspey had a tame grouse, you know, which could say seven words.'

'What were they?'

'"Double whisky, please", and "Ich bin ein Berliner."'

'That doesn't prove intelligence.' 'Well, it was four more words than the Earl could say. It was a family joke whether the Earl had a tame grouse or the grouse had a tame earl.'

They fell silent. In the woods a distant murmuring noise could be heard, so soft you weren't even sure there was a noise there at all. It was the sort of noise you get from a distant sea or, alternatively, the moment just before the enemy charges. The two men's nerves were as sharp as raw rhubarb.

'Do you know what worries me?' said McAllister suddenly. 'What worries me is that every 12 August, regular as clock-work, we've gone in and cleaned 'em out. It would be a singularly stupid bird that didn't tumble to this sooner or later and act accordingly.'

'How do you mean, act accordingly?' 'Try and wipe us out on 11 August. In other words, tonight.'

They stared out again through the gloom, though less was now visible than at any time. The thought that, at any moment, thousands of grouse might bear down on them, whirring madly and beating at them with those savage claws, was unbearable. A single bird suddenly came out of the dark air and Duncan Wood swung up his gun, but McAllister laid a hand on his arm. It was only an owl.

'Steady on, old boy. You've been too long in the butts. It's getting to you. The reinforcements will be here tomorrow.'

Duncan Wood laughed savagely. 'Reinforcements? Japanese financiers, English football managers and Belgian politicians? Dear God, can they not send us any good shots up the line these days? Last year we even had an American who shot himself in the foot.'

'If we can hold on until they get here, we'll be all right.'

Somewhere away on the hills a single cottage light flickered and went out. The country folk would be getting an early night and staying well clear on the morrow. Experience had told them it would be death not to.

'I wonder if it will always go on like this?' said McAllister suddenly. 'Will grouse and man always be at war? Will we always have this carnage? I sometimes dream of the day when man and grouse live at peace and call each other brother bird.'

'Brother bird?' said Duncan Wood, amazed. 'Have ye gone mad? The grouse will not rest until every man has been swept off the earth, or at least from this part of Glen Usk.'

'That is what we have always been told. Yet I remember a tame grouse that used to be with Mrs Robertson of Glen Killin. I was talking to this grouse one day, and he told me that he couldn't understand man's murderous hatred of grouse.'

'Us? Hatred? Murderers? You've been talking to too many tame grouse. It's the grouse who hate us, as well ye ken. You wouldn't be a secret grouse-lover by any chance, McAllister?'

It was the worst insult Duncan Wood could think of. It was the worst McAllister knew as well. He flushed and said nothing.

Out there, in no man's land, nothing moved in the air at all. The two men never thought of looking down at the ground. If they had, they might have seen several hundred hand-picked grouse creeping through the heather on a special 11 August daredevil mission. Duncan Wood and McAllister never knew what hit them, and the reinforcements had not the faintest idea what could have happened when they found them the next morning, dead, neatly plucked and hanging upside down from a branch.

A Novel for Starters

GOING away on holiday soon? Then you'll be needing a holiday novel. Trouble is, holiday novels are far too long and heavy, so here today is a complete holiday novel which you can cut out now and read later. No, don't read on now. Wait until your hols to read . . .

The Cutting Edge

Edward was bored. He had been on holiday for four days and he was bored already. Every day he went out on the beach and the sunshine poured down and he rubbed cream on himself and lay cooking himself. He felt like a sausage. He was beginning to look like a sausage.

Right now he was bored because the waiter had taken his order and hadn't come back with his lunch. If only he had a book with him.

And then he suddenly remembered; somewhere in his wallet he had a newspaper cutting, something he'd torn out of *The Independent* which promised to be a complete novel and which, feeling like a complete idiot, he had actually brought with him.

He opened his wallet and unfolded the crumpled bit of paper, then, flattening it on the table between his knife and fork . . .

'Excuse me . . .'

Edward looked up. Two tall men wearing suits and sunglasses were standing over him.

'You will come with us, please.'

'I'm waiting for my lunch.'

'It will not take a moment. Come, please.'

Not knowing quite why, he followed them out to the car park, to a large BMW into which they unceremoniously bundled him before driving away at high speed down the coast road. 'What the hell . . .' said Edward. The man sitting next to him turned and punched him hard on the jaw. Edward could feel the blood trickling down his lip and licked the warm, slightly salty wetness. It looked like being the only lunch he was going to get.

'Don't ask questions,' said the man, 'because we don't know the answers. All we know is that we were sent to pick up a contact, whom we would know because he was reading a newspaper cutting. We are taking you to Mr Henderson and you will hand over the merchandise to him.'

'But I haven't got any . . .'

110

The man hit him again and Edward decided to stay quiet. After 20 minutes spent at about 70 mph, they turned into the drive of a large villa hidden by high walls and he was dragged into the presence of a man he supposed must be Henderson.

'Welcome, Mr Nossiter,' said Henderson, a suave man with Gucci shoes and Saatchi and Saatchi spectacles. 'Please hand it over.'

'I am not called Nossiter, and I do not have any . . .'

Mr Henderson hit him, hard.

'Look!' said Edward, losing his temper. 'I am getting fed up being hit by everyone and I want to be taken back because my lunch will be getting cold.'

'Of course,' said Henderson. 'As soon as you have handed over the secrets. Not till then.'

Edward was locked up in a small room containing a bed and a table. The next time the door opened, the most beautiful blonde he had ever seen slipped inside and locked it behind her.

'We haven't got much time, Nossiter,' she said.

'Time for what?'

'To make mad, passionate love, of course.'

They made mad, passionate love on the bed. Then they made mad, passionate love on the table. Then she rolled over invitingly on the floor.

'That's all very well,' said Edward, 'but I wish someone would tell me . . .'

She rose suddenly, as if she heard something, and ran out of the room, dropping a pistol as she fled. Moments later Mr Henderson appeared in the doorway. Edward shot him. Then he ran down the passage and out of the house, where he found the BMW sitting unattended with the keys in the ignition.

His heart pounding, he started the engine and drove at breakneck speed back along the coast road to the restaurant where, just as he regained his table, the waiter turned up with his paella.

Beside his place lay the cutting. Edward put it away, unread. He suddenly realized what had been happening. He had filled in the time, not by reading a holiday novel, but by *being* in a holiday novel. He dug into his paella, thinking that his holiday was beginning to pick up after all.

(Pretty exciting, eh? More complete holiday novels coming soon.)

Down and Out in Yokelshire

IF CONSCIENCE doth make cowards of us all, I wonder what social conscience doth to us? In my case, it madeth a fool out of me, and I hope this instructive little tale will be a warning to others.

Some time ago I moved from London to the depths of the country in order to commune with nature and reap the benefits of lower house prices. I was very anxious not to injure the community I was joining, in the way that the Isle of Dogs was apparently being altered by the influx of yuppies. One East Ender had recently been quoted as saying: 'We were told we were going to share in all these great new computerized, hightech jobs, but all we're offered is two hours of cleaning in the morning for the yuppies' wives. No wonder we're on the flaming warpath!'

I remembered this remark with a social pang when, several days after we arrived in the village, my wife said: 'Look, we really are going to need a cleaner. Couldn't you put a card in the Post Office window asking for one? I'm sure one of the locals would love to do a couple of hours.'

'I think they'd probably prefer to have work as computer operators, dear,' I said mildly.

'We haven't got any opening for computer operators in this house,' she said, less than mildly. 'Just go and put that card in the window.'

The card I eventually put in the window read:
Wanted, Cleaner, For Two Hours Work Daily: Must Have Thorough Computer and Electronics Training.'

There was only one applicant for the job. He was a pleasant young man called Stephen who had done a course in computer work and was now looking for a temporary job. I offered him the choice between ironing and vacuum cleaning. By the end of the morning he had done both. I thanked him very much, paid him and fired him.

'You *fired* him?' said my wife. 'Why on earth . . .?'

'Because he charged me £45 an hour,' I said. 'He maintained that was basic computer operator's pay. Basic pay, that is. He also charged VAT, travelling expenses . . .'

'Serve you right for your bleeding heart advert,' said the wife. 'I suggest you pop down to the Post Office and rephrase it, pronto.'

I did. As fairly as I could, I rewrote it to read: Computer-trained person needed for light cleaning duties, at normal cleaning rates, repeat normal cleaning rates.' There was one applicant for the for job. It was Stephen again.

'Not many cleaners in the area just now, I'm afraid,' he said. 'When can I start?'

'You can start any time at £3 an hour,' I said strictly. 'No more computer workers' rates, is that understood?'

'Quite understood.'

I didn't see much of Stephen for the next month, but my wife gave me to understand that his work was of a very high order. Stephen, she said, had been telling her all about his plans to set up a computerized cleaning lady service for country areas. He was, she said, a lad full of ooomph and zip and go, qualities which, she implied, were absent from me.

She then handed me this bill for the month. It came to £900.

'This is impossible,' I said.

'It includes the hire of his cleaning equipment,' she said. 'That comes very expensive. He is also getting his cleaning operation computerized, which comes expensive as well.'

'Well, I'm not paying that bill.'

'And he has come up with a wonderful idea,' she continued. 'He has discovered a quite legal way of avoiding tax and national insurance for cleaning people.'

'Oh?' I said, interested despite myself.

'Time-sharing! When the cleaner comes in of a morning, you lease him your house on time-share basis. When the cleaner leaves, you get it back. So, during cleaning hours, the cleaner is cleaning his own house and doesn't have to be paid tax! And his wages come as a rent rebate! It's a brilliant idea!'

I had to admit it was. I even agreed to try the scheme out with us. But somewhere along the line I must have misunderstood the contract, because now I find that my wife is living in the house with Stephen, the handsome young computer expert, and I have been ousted from my home, and am forced to live in a tiny cottage down the road.

Times are hard at the moment. The other day I answered a card in the Post Office window offering occasional cleaning work. I find I am now on Stephen's computerized books. Honestly, I think we yuppies deserve a better deal from the local yokel than a couple of hours' cleaning work now and then.

113

Take the Money and Stay

DO YOU ever think about bank clerks?

Yes, you sometimes push cheques through a grille at them, and get money back from them, and occasionally you might even have a muttered conversation with them, but do you ever think about what it's *like* to be a bank clerk?

For instance, you must have noticed that they now work behind such thick panes of glass and have so little access to your side of the world that when you want to speak to them, you have to lean down and talk into the little aperture through which the money is squeezed. Most exchanges between you and a bank clerk go like this:

Clerk: Howja banja monkey?

You: Pardon?

Clerk: Howja banja monkey?

You: I'm sorry, I can't hear what you're saying.

Clerk *(leaning forward, face sideways into the cheque slit):* How would you like the money?

You: Oh. As it comes, please.

Asking a bank customer how he wants it is a bit like asking a pub customer whether he wants a straight glass or a handle. A waste of time. The customer, 99 times out of 100, could not care less. The question is asked only to satisfy the man behind the counter, not the customer and, in the case of the bank cashier, is asked to establish some form of human contact.

Because a bank cashier is a prisoner.

He is trapped behind his plate glass window. Look upwards, and you will see they have installed spikes to stop him climbing out. Look at his face and tell me if you do not see the face of a prisoner. Do you never feel the urge to say to a bank clerk:

'How are they treating you?'

Or: 'Do you know when they are going to let you out?'

When this idea is first put to them, people generally chuckle and say: 'That's ridiculous – they let bank clerks out at lunch-time for a start.'

When have you ever seen a bank clerk out at lunch-time?

'Maybe so,' people reply, 'but bank workers go home at the end of the day like everyone else.' But is this really so? What happens when a bank's doors close at 3.30 pm? Do you see the workers pack up and go home? No. Your last glimpse as the doors clang shut is of

114

their pale faces, in sad rows behind the plate-glass windows, sitting there as if they were doomed to stay all night. Which is exactly what they are going to do. And which explains why, when banks open in the morning, they are all there already.

Nobody ever sees a bank clerk leave or arrive. And this is not surprising, as they all live in small dormitories out of sight.

That is why the Bank Liberation Movement asks for your urgent support.

Next time you are in a bank, look at the man who hovers over the door at closing time, preparing to lock up for the rest of the day, and then after locking time letting the last few customers out. Ask yourself if he looks like a man who has been put there to be nice to customers *or more like a man whose job it is to keep the cashiers from making a bolt for freedom.* If he was meant to be nice to customers, wouldn't they have chosen someone a bit – well, nicer?

Next time you use a service till, ask yourself why some seem very quick and some seem slow. Ask yourself why the machine almost seems to be making its mind up sometimes. And ask yourself if it is not possible that the machine is only a front for some poor, tired, overworked bank clerk on the other side of the wall who is handling your request as fast as he can.

That's nonsense, people say. Bank clerks operating service tills? It's all done by machinery!

Have you ever seen the machinery?

OK. But it couldn't be worked by bank clerks. They don't keep bank clerks in all night!

Don't they? We've already suggested very strongly that they do, and we think that you are beginning to believe us.

That's why we in the Bank Liberation Movement desperately need your support. We are starting to make well-planned raids on local branches to liberate these poor captives and the cruel amounts of money they have to handle. You may even have seen some of our operatives in action, dressed in their distinctive face stockings and overcoats, as they go about their mercy work, bustling in and out of banks before the authorities realize that a rescue bid is taking place.

Will *you* support the Bank Liberation Movement in our work? Not by sending us money – we have plenty of that – but simply by standing aside when you see us on an operation, and not trying to interfere. And if the police should later ask you questions – well, mum's the word.

OK? Bless you!

Big Fight in East Londinium

THE recent discovery of an amphitheatre in London brings to 10 the number of Roman stadiums known to have existed in Britain, with another 10 suspected. Even more amazingly, a fragment of a conversation between two Romano-British sports fans has also been uncovered recently. Here it is . . .

Publius: . . . and two Saturdays ago I was at Viroconium.

Junius: Over towards Wales?

Publius: Right. Or Gallia, as we call it. We've got a little holiday villa in Gallia, so I went to see if it were all right. The Gallia Liberation Army have been trying to burn it down for years. Anyway, I had to come back via Viroconium, so I thought I'd take in the gladiatorial show on the Saturday.

Junius: What's the standard of fighting like in the provinces?

Publius: Well, you remember the fight spectacular we went to two months ago, down East Londinium?

Junius: How could I forget? That was the night Thrasimodo, the Terrible Thracian, carved up Desperandum, the Dacian Ace. A massacre, it was. Blood everywhere. Great fight. Well, stands to reason, being a grudge match like that. We all knew one of them had to die. I was a bit sorry it had to be Desperandum. I loved the way he waggled his sword and screamed.

Publius: Is this my story or yours?

Junius: Sorry. Carry on.

Publius: Anyway, who do you think was top of the bill at Viroconium?

Junius: Search me. Balbus, the Blond Beast? No, hold on, he was killed last time out against Molo the Mad Christian.

Publius: It was Thrasimodo the Terrible Thracian.

Junius: Blimey – recovered from his wounds already?

Publius: Against Desperandum, the Dacian Ace.

Junius: WHAT? But he's dead.

Publius: Nevertheless, I saw him fighting on Saturday last.

Junius: You saw a dead man fighting?

Publius: I did. Not only that, but I saw them fight exactly the same fight, blow for blow, with the same end, when Desperandum gets hacked to bits.

Junius: That's crazy. I saw him die already.

Publius: That's what I said. I got up and shouted: 'I've seen this man die already! This is not natural! The gods are mocked!'

Junius: Good for you. What happened then?

Publius: A couple of heavies leapt on me and took me off to the manager's office, to have a talk with the boss. He said to me: 'You're spoiling people's fun. Would you like your money back before we throw you out?'

Junius: The nerve!

Publius: So I told him that I had been at the night in East Londinium where Desperandum had previously been killed and how did he explain that, also how did he explain the fight going the same way both times? 'Listen, kid,' he said, 'that fight has gone the same way 10 times and we've still got 10 stadiums to go.'

Junius: I don't understand.

Publius: Nor did I. So he explained. Apparently all these Saturday afternoon fights are fixed. They plan the whole fight in advance. And the death is just fixed to look like a death.

Junius: But the blood?

Publius: Red paint.

Junius: The severed limbs?

Publius: Imitation. He showed me. He even introduced me to Desperandum.

Junius: But why do they bother?

Publius: Saves a lot of money if you keep your gladiators from one fight to the next. And when you've got a chain of 20 amphitheatres round Britain, you can guarantee a fresh audience every time. Nobody will spot the deception. Nearly nobody. They were just unlucky with me.

Junius: This is terrible.

Publius: Balbus the Blond Beast was on the bill as well, only he's Africanus the Black Barbarian now.

Junius: I shall never go to another fight show.

Publius: Most of the swords aren't real. They're wood painted silver.

Junius: I don't see the point of a game if no one gets killed.

Publius: He's working on a new game now, where teams of men kick a bladder full of air from one end of the stadium to the other, and back again.

Junius: And then kill each other?

Publius: They pretend to, but mostly they kick the bladder.

Junius: This is the end of sport as we know it. Once you stop people killing each other, the whole fun goes out of sport. If this goes on, you mark my words, audiences will rise up in fury and destroy our amphitheatres, just crush them into little bits. And one day in the future people will find the ruins of our amphitheatres and they will . . . *And that is where the fragment ends. Sorry.*

The Prevention of Cruelty
to Dandelions

'HAVE you ever been into the fields, armed with a basket and sharp knife, to gather the small green tender shoots of the first dandelion and turned it on your return into a delicate salad?' inquires a recent issue of *Country Homes and Interiors*. 'Eggs are the usual accompaniment – quail's eggs, looking like painted Easter eggs, seem to fit the atmosphere of the month.'

How the memories came flooding back! In the old days, my father and I often sallied forth into the fields at sparrowfart – his bucolic word for dawn – in search of the cunning dandelion. I would be armed with a sharp knife and basket, while he liked to take a couple of rifles, a coil of rope, a clutch of hand grenades and a water cannon. We were usually accompanied by our pet quail's eggs, Hubert and Alphonse, who would gambol along behind us on the end of a string or, more usually, sit snug and warm in my father's pocket.

'A dandelion can turn savagely on a man,' my father told me, 'so we must go quietly if we are to beard the dandelion in his den at chickenyawn.'

'Chickenyawn?' I said wonderingly.

''Tis an old country phrase used as a mild alternative to sparrow-fart,' he said, and suddenly he was off into the undergrowth followed by Hubert and Alphonse. There were great thrashings around, several shots were fired and he came back clutching a huge dandelion, freshly throttled.

'Got the little beggar,' he grinned.

'Shall we take it home to cook, father?'

'We shall do no such thing,' frowned my father, his face darkening, until, after a minute, he looked very like Nat King Cole. I leant forward and adjusted the brightness control. 'I shall not rest until I have rid the country of this noxious pest, but I would not sink so far as to eat my enemy.'

Depending on the month, we might leave the quail's eggs at home and take some other pair for a stroll. In autumn, when fresh ones were scarce, we often took out a pair of puffin's eggs, blown and hand-painted. Father had picked these up in a local antique shop. Then he had slipped them into his pocket and walked out without paying. As a simple countryman, he distrusted the use of money and, finding barter cumbersome, preferred to steal.

'Have to be up at cloudbirth to get the best of me,' he would say, winking sagely.

'Cloudbirth, father?'

'Aye, an old country phrase sometimes used instead of chicken-yawn. My God, look on 'em! Millions of 'em!'

This was usually a sign that he had spotted dandelion seeds floating through the air, which to him looked like a mass airborne invasion of tiny parachutists. He would turn his water cannon on them and slaughter thousands at a time. Out of respect for the enemy, he sometimes arranged mass burials of these tiny, bedraggled corpses. Friends would wonder why our lawn was covered with small white, unmarked crosses. My father would wonder why dandelions grew in such profusion round the crosses, but in many ways he was a simple man.

In later life he grew too weak to go out hunting, and he was never the same again after he sat on Hubert and Alphonse. He started training two young plover's eggs, Norbert and Rodolphe, but his heart wasn't in it.

'I hate to think of all that country wisdom passing away with you,' I said.

'Nay, lad,' he said. 'Have I not taught you how to creep up behind a dandelion wi' sharp knife and cut his throat?'

'I am a city boy now, father. In the city, they look after dandelions and take them home to turn into delicate salads.'

His face went crimson with fury, clashing violently with the lilac curtains; then he went pale with the effort, harmonizing with the decor once more.

'When I die, you will find all the country knowledge you need under my bed,' he whispered.

And so I did. There he had hidden piles of magazines such as *Country Fabrics, Salads and Sofas, Comfy Cottage Living, Country Talk, Loos and Lampshades*. He had marked one article, entitled 'Sparrowfart and Other Country Names For Dawn'. Another, cut out and yellowing, was headed: 'Dandelion Shoots: All You Need To Know'. Poor father. Never the best of readers, he had misread this to assume that dandelions were there to be shot.

'He was a true countryman,' I said to my mother.

'Aye,' she said. 'He would believe anything he was told.'

'Mother!' I said. 'You had to get up at foxbath to get the best of father.'

'Foxbath?' she said. 'Oh no, don't you start!'

119

Marcel Proust: Sponsored by Madeleine Biscuits

IF MAGAZINES, papers, radio and television thrive on advertising, why are books the lone exception? Such is the thinking of Whittle Communications, an innovative American publisher. And being American, it has gone ahead and done it; nine well-known US writers, including J K Galbraith, are at this very moment writing books which will be full of ads.

I have mixed feelings about this. Yes, I think it is a good idea. No, I don't think it goes nearly far enough. I suppose now is the time for me to come out in the open and confess that I had this idea years ago, but I went much further than Whittle Communications. I felt that the advertising should not occur in a book in little pockets, like lumps in a white sauce, but blend smoothly into the book.

'I don't see quite how you could do that,' said the publisher I approached at the time.

'Easy,' I told him. 'When an advertiser buys space in a novel, you make sure that his product is used by the hero or one of the sympathetic characters.'

'Mmmm,' said the publisher, greed lighting up those amiable eyes. 'But won't it cause a terrible fuss?'

'Who's to know if we don't tell them?'

We started small, with a crime series in which the likeable inspector had a taste for a certain cigar, aperitif and brand of tea. He stayed in a certain hotel and drove a certain make of car. I'd mention their names now, but they aren't paying me any more. It was hard to tell how much it affected sales, but it can't have hurt, and the manufacturers were absurdly pleased to see their names in print in literature.

The next stage came when we were approached by a paint manufacturer who offered us money to make the inspector a D I Y enthusiast, always repainting his house. This didn't fit in with his character, we said. All right, said the paint people, why not have a spot of our paint as the vital clue on the murderer's clothes?

This made more sense. And for quite a large sum of money, we ensured that the forensic scientist picked out a minute dot of paint on a bloodstained overall and said: 'This proves that your suspect *was* involved in those house repairs four years ago; this is Lords Paint, which lasts better than any other paint, without chipping or wearing. And this is their Cornflower Blue range which was replaced by Azure Mediterranean four years ago.'

Well, once it was established that the manufacturer could be in at the planning stage of a novel and shape its plot, a whole new world opened up. Tourist boards came to us to pay for thrillers to be set in their country. Whole professions paid for their calling to be given a more glamorous image; if you read a thriller in which the detective is an accountant or in which an advertising executive turns detective, you'll know why.

How far has this spread throughout the publishing world? Were the Swiss hotel people behind the setting of *Hotel du Lac*? Did Kingsley Amis get a hefty subsidy from the drinks people for all the swilling that goes on in *The Old Devils*? I honestly don't know but it all fits in with what we started.

The next big step was adverse advertising, which worked like this. If a character in a novel was a building society manager, to whom the heroine went for help, you would imagine that some building society or other had put a few thousand into the novel. To begin with, he is all smiles and brotherly love; then he gradually starts developing feelings for the heroine which go beyond the professional. He takes her out to dinner. He makes suggestions. When she reacts indignantly, he points out that the way her money is tied up with him she can hardly afford to refuse.

This loathsome man can hardly have been paid for by the building societies. No, indeed not. The money has come from the clearing banks. Some big high-street bank has paid good money to see building societies discredited in a work of art. It's called adverse advertising and it's very effective.

The latest development involves advertisers paying to get into rewritten classics. I have already seen a sly rewrite of a Sherlock Holmes story in which Watson guesses that Holmes has been somewhere strange because he is smoking an unusual tobacco. 'Instead of,' adds Watson, 'your usual . . .' – and then he names a Victorian-sounding tobacco.

This reference cannot promote sales. It merely mentions the advertiser's name attached to a fictitious product. But after all, we already have vanity publishing which exists only to puff up the writer's ego and empty his pocket. Why not, similarly, vanity advertising?

A Murder on the Aubusson Express

TODAY – a great new unabridged 1930s detective story!
'CHECKLAND!'

The voice of the Duke of Hussey rang out through his ancestral home.

'Yes, your Grace?'

As usual, Checkland appeared silently at his elbow, as if from no-where. The Duke found Checkland's omnipresence very reassuring and at the same time rather disturbing: it was as if, every time one prayed, one could distinctly hear God saying: 'Yes?'

'Ah, Checkland, I hope you didn't mind my shouting. Thought you might be up in that top room of yours, with all your radio and television sets. All working, are they?'

Checkland might be the Duke's man by trade, but by inclination he was a tinkerer with wires, tubes and glowing screens. Well, if it kept him happy.

'Yes, your Grace, thank you. Did you need help of some kind?'

'I'd certainly appreciate your advice, Checkland. We've had a mes-sage from old Lady Rees-Mogg this morning, and she's in a fair old state, going on about murder most vile. She wonders if we could pop round and take a look. Specially asked for you by name, as a matter of fact.'

Lady Rees-Mogg, one of his Somerset neighbours, was a dear old thing who often rang up to complain about this and that, but this was the first time she had ever reported a murder. He thought of himself as a gentleman detective, even if he dimly realized that this was a contradiction in terms – after all, a gentleman would not investigate a murder; he would carry on as if nothing had happened.

'If you're free to come over, Checkland, I'd appreciate it. I'm just ringing to make sure she's in. Hello?'

'Hello?' came the unmistakable tones of Lady Rees-Mogg. 'Is that Barclays Bank? Look, I'm absolutely furious . . .'

'No, no, it's Hussey here,' said the Duke hastily. 'Don't move a thing, Wilhemina. We'll be right over.'

Ten minutes later he and Checkland were at the front door of Antiquaria Hall, the Rees-Mogg home.

'If you've come to sell books, it's round the back,' said the house-keeper, Mrs Variorum. 'Oh, sorry, your Grace – I'll take you straight to Lady Rees-Mogg. She's on the phone.'

Lady Rees-Mogg was, as it turned out, still talking to what she imagined to be the Duke of Hussey. The Duke smiled.

'Tell us all about your murder, Wilhemina.'

Lady Rees-Mogg, puzzled, put down the phone and launched into a rambling tale about the murder she had witnessed the night before. A man had been killed . . . run over . . . perfectly foul . . . blood all over the mudguard . . .

'Why didn't you ring and tell us last night, Wilhemina?'

'I felt like an early bed, Hussey, these murders always make me feel tired.'

'Hmm,' said the Duke, nonplussed. 'And where did it take place exactly?'

'Right here in my drawing-room,' said her ladyship, surprised. 'Where else did you think?'

A hit-and-run accident. On the carpet of the drawing-room. The Duke felt totally baffled. He glanced helplessly at Checkland, who took over effortlessly.

'Was this about 9.37 pm, your ladyship?'

'Yes, about then.'

'Was the car a large beige Lagonda, driven by a man in goggles with a masked lady at his side?'

'Yes, it was, as a matter of fact.'

As always, the Duke of Hussey felt quite overawed by Checkland's omniscience.

'On BBC2?'

'Yes, I believe so.'

Checkland turned to the Duke: 'It's the one of these new television programmes about 1930s country house crime, sir. There's a lot of it about, all nostalgia and 78 rpm discs.'

'But if it was only on television, why did you call us over, Wilhemina?' said the Duke.

'That's the *point*, Hussey. If you show things like this on television, pretty soon people all over the country will be hiring Lagondas and going out to run over people they don't like. It was horrible, horrible, horrible . . . Luckily I recorded it, and I was able to watch the car accident over and over again till I felt quite sick. Oh, *do* something about it, Hussey!'

Hussey patted her knee and promised he would. On their way back, he turned to Checkland and said: 'Thanks for driving me over, Checkland. Bit unnecessary as it turned out.'

'Always glad to be on hand, sir,' said Checkland.

It was impossible to tell, from his features, what he was thinking.

The Life of Dorset Maugham

'DO YOU know why we allow politicians and soldiers to get away with such boring and self-glorifying memoirs?' my publisher asked me one day about 10 years ago. 'Because they hand their copy in on time. This never happens with real writers. Real writers happily go past the deadline by months, even years, and give us all heart attacks. But an old general or prime minister hands his manuscript in exactly when it is asked for. This gives us a thrill which not even their dead prose can totally spoil.'

I knew what was coming next. He was going to ask me where my book was.

'And where is your book, by the way?'

'I haven't finished the research yet, actually.'

I hadn't started it either. In those days I was quite incapable of getting a book in on time, or late, or at all. All I was good at was being promising, and showering charm on publishers. But that day the charm had run out, and it was ultimatum time.

'I'm going to give you one last chance. A famous author of ours has just died and we need to do a quick biography of him. You are the only decent writer available, reliable or not. I can give you five or six months. If you do it, I can forgive you your past sins. If you don't, I can make sure you never do another book for anyone.'

There was nothing for it but to buckle down to the quick life and times of – well, let's call him Dorset Maugham. He wasn't as famous as Somerset, but he had an enormous following and the biography would establish me again.

I quite enjoyed the research, or at least meeting all Dorset's relations. Dorset had been a bad-tempered, mean old bird, and his relatives, mostly jovial types, were not disposed to cover up his shortcomings. In fact, I was soon put in possession of the real skeleton in Dorset's wardrobe: his mistress. This was something of a scoop, as none of the gossip writers had ever got on to it, so as soon as I had secured the address of Julia Thursday (her name), I was off like a shot.

She lived in one of the few parts of England which are not yet in the London commuter belt, South Yorkshire. On the train journey I met Thurlow Banster. Do you remember Banster? Grand old critic, regular on radio, lead reviewer in the *Sunday Blah*, etc, and a man with much influence. I introduced myself. He had heard of me, but thought I had given up writing. He was nearly right.

'I much admire your books, sir,' I told him. It was true. I hadn't read them, but I much admired them. 'And what brings you away from London?'

His next words froze my blood.

'Oh, I'm engaged on a quick biography of old Dorset Maugham. I'm off to see his mistress, the fair Julia.'

Not only did I have a rival in what had seemed a clear field, but he knew of the mystery mistress. Knew her well too, from the sound of it. To make it worse, he had an appointment with her, whereas I was going strictly on spec. When he left the train at the other end and jumped into a taxi I felt that the lifeline to freedom and solvency which the Dorset Maugham book represented had been cut off.

I also felt an irrational surge of hatred for Thurlow Banster as I trudged the long walk towards the house (he had taken the only local taxi) and when he suddenly appeared round a bend coming the other way he seemed to embody all that stood between me and success. Several thoughts ran through my mind at top speed. I had not told Banster that I was doing Dorset's life. He could not have told Julia Thursday that I was coming. Nobody knew that Banster and I had ever met. We were totally alone and unwatched. And Banster must not be allowed to live . . .

Do you remember the fuss 10 years ago about Thurlow Banster's disappearance? Then later the headlines: 'Famous Critic Found Strangled In Lonely Wood'? All my doing, I'm afraid. Still, there was a happy ending to the story. They never found the murderer and my book on Dorset Maugham did extremely well. I even got to talk to Julia Thursday eventually, and a most valuable series of talks it was too. Among other things she revealed that she had not always been faithful to old Dorset. She had in fact had a long-time lover. I wonder if you can guess who. Yes, old Thurlow Banster. Curious coincidence, *n'est-ce pas*?

Not the only one, either. My publisher later offered me the chance to write another top-selling instant biog. The life of the late Thurlow Banster, in fact. I felt bound to turn it down. As I told him, I was a sensitive man and I didn't feel quite up to dealing with the distasteful events in the last chapter.

And Now, a Choice of Lord's Prayers

DEFENDERS of the new Lord's Prayer tell us that the word 'sins' has been put in instead of 'trespasses', because people simply don't use words like trespass any more. What they don't tell us is why the word 'hallowed' is still in, a word which has not been used in everyday conversation since 1850. No, the fact of the matter is that the new Lord's Prayer is a muddle and needs to be replaced.

Not by another Lord's Prayer, though, but by *lots* of Lord's Prayers, to give the consumer the choice which he finds in every other area of life. I am quite happy to give the Church a lead in this matter, so I have been programming my computer to produce versions of the famous prayer to suit different kinds of people. For instance, it is said that children have difficulty identifying with the Lord's Prayer, so I asked the computer to try one suitable for a 12-year-old. Here is the result.

'Dear God, I hope you are well. I am well. I hope everything is all right in Heaven. It is fine on earth. Thank you for giving us our food today, and I quite understand if that is the best you can do. I am sorry about the bad things I have done, but you should see the bad things that other people have done! Still, I will not mention any names. Please keep me good or at least out of trouble. Well, I think that's everything. PS: Thanks for everything. More please.'

At the other end of the spectrum from the little child is the estate agent, but even for him the computer readily provided a suitable Lord's Prayer.

'Dear Resident, Living as you do in a highly desirable area, we are respectfully here to do your bidding. If you wish to get in touch with us today or at any time in the future in order to discuss a mutual arrangement for the subsequent handling of your property or anyone's property, we believe we can offer you a fault-free service as far as is possible. We will be guided by your wishes at all times, for which purpose we are open 24 hours a day.'

Here is a version of the prayer for a health food person.

'Dear Godparent, I hope everything is totally together with you, up there. Thank you for making everything pure and organic, and I hope between us we can eliminate all additives, preservatives, etc. Give us today a large wholemeal and some tofu for Friday, and please overlook any hassles we may have causd, as we shall do the same. Don't let us be tempted by any butter, cream or white things, OK! This prayer comes on 100 per cent recycled paper.

One for a yuppy . . .

'Open new file headed GOD. Message to God – greetings in the fast lane. Anything you want, you just say, we will have it on line for you. Your office or ours, it makes no difference. Just give me a couple of sandwiches at lunchtime, and the rest of the day is yours. I might cut a few corners, but who doesn't? Thanks for the house, car, wife, etc, and I realize it won't last for ever, unlike you, but I have to rush now. We must have lunch some time.'

We even tried one for a street-cred youth, though the computer struggled a little.

'All right, John? All right. Everything all right up there? Fine down here. Everything's cool with me, if it's cool with you. You make sure I get what I need, plus enough bread, and I'll handle it. Yeah, I can handle it. Course I can handle it! All right, all right – with *your* help I can handle it. Don't be heavy. I don't want a heavy number. All right, cool. Keep in touch, yeah?'

And finally, because they always get in on the act sooner or later, a Lord's Prayer for lawyers.

'It is a great pleasure to address your Godship in this court or any higher one, may it please your Godship, to whom I defer in this matter as indeed I do in all others. May I humbly say how grateful I am to your Godship for the granting of daily costs? May I also beg your Godship's forbearance and forgiveness in advance for any transgressions I may commit here or elsewhere, as I am sure I would grant to anyone else, and I hope with your Godship's guidance to avoid all fault. Please carry on, your Godship, and don't mind me.'

If you want our computer to give you a personal Lord's Prayer, just get in touch.

For the Man Who Has Everything but Can't Find It

EVER been secretly sorry that books don't have a fall-out sales catalogue of trendy electronic and black leather gimmicks? Weep no more. Here it is.

* LUMINOUS GOLF COURSE.

Bought a luminous golf ball recently? The one that lets you play after dark? And then found, naturally, that you couldn't see where to aim it? What you need is the new Indie Luminous Golf Course. After sundown it comes magically alight with soft phosphorescent tints, so that the whole of your evening round is dreamily lit in a choice of three hues: Hoylake Hazel, St Andrews' Salmon or Golden Wentworth. And, of course, with the magical glow of the Indie Luminous Course, you won't be needing those expensive luminous golf balls any more!

* CORDLESS TELEPHONE ANSWERING DEVICE.

You're sitting on the homeward-bound Intercity from London to Bristol. It's been a hard day – you've motivated half a sales force and fired the other half, and now you're feeling tired. Suddenly the phone rings, just when you were dropping off. Maybe it's the wife, wanting to know if she should activate the luminous golf course for your evening round. Maybe it's a wrong number. But with a cordless phone tucked into your jacket, you've got to answer it, just in case it's important . . . Not any more! The new Indie Answerer takes the message in your armpit while you sleep. It gives golfing instructions to your wife, and fires any salesmen who happen to call in. And it wakes you up five minutes before you get to Bristol!

* IMPERSONAL STEREO.

You're sitting next to some fat sleeping businessman on the Intercity train. His cordless phone answering device keeps clicking on and off, as his wife keeps ringing him to tell him his luminous golf course is on fire. It's driving you mad. How do you get your own back? Easy! You put on your Indie Wakeman! This is a personal-type stereo which makes lots of drumming and bass guitar noises for anyone sitting within 10 yards – but is completely silent inside. Yes, the music only plays for other people and you can hear nothing! You'll drive that businessman round the bend and sleep like a baby yourself.

* ELECTRONIC WELSH FIRE ALARM.

Got a little Welsh weekend cottage? Haven't we all? Worried stiff it might get singed during the week? Aren't we all? Well, no, actually, we're not – not if we've got an Indie Welsh Fire Alarm fitted! The heat sensors in this fragile device detect fire immediately and trigger off your bleep hundreds of miles away, so that you can ring the Llanyblodwen police and fire brigade from your seat in your Intercity train and get them round pronto to the cottage.

* EXERCISE BIKE VIDEO.

You've been pedalling away on your executive exercise bike for 10 minutes. You can feel the muscles in your legs working. And one thought is uppermost in your mind: God, this is boring! But it needn't be, not with our Glories of Britain video to watch on your new handlebar monitor screen. As you pedal, see the heritage landscape roll past, just like a real cyclist – the luminous golf courses, the blazing Welsh cottages, the sacked sales force roaming aimlessly up and down the M1 – and look, isn't that a hapless railway passenger with his excruciating Indie Impersonal Stereo being flung from the train window?

* RAPID BLEEP SORTER.

You are woken from your sleep by an electronic noise. But what is it? The cordless phone answerer, the Welsh fire bleep, the bike video timer, your singing key ring, your luminous golf course remote switch or just the bloke next door with his bloody stereo? What you need is the Indie Electronic Bleep Sorter – one glance at its screen will tell you which device is bleeping for you.

* BLEEP STRESS PLANNER. Modern doctors think that too many electronic devices can actually cause more stress than they alleviate. They bring problems closer to you, turn every little noise into a possible crisis. What does this mean? Well, it probably means you'll drop down dead much sooner than you expected. And that means there'll be an awful lot of engagements in your personal planner that you're going to miss. But don't worry. The New Indie Stress Planner has a built-in sensor that can actually tell when you're dead – *and which will then actually delete all unfilled obligations from the planner, so that it can be used again!* The de luxe version will also deactivate your credit cards, activate an alarm on your kidney donor card – and bleep your next of kin to tell them you're dead! You can't afford to be without it.

A Recorded Message from Death

A COMPLETE novel for businessmen today. It's written as a multi-choice questionnaire in which you have to guess what the hero will do next. Or, as you high-fliers would say, evaluate his action potential. So here we go with:

To Make a Killing

YOU are Wesley Brockbank, head of a huge firm called Webro International. Webro is very rich indeed and so are you. You are not entirely without sentiment, however; once a year you go to lay flowers on the grave of your ex-chauffeur, who died in an accident while you were both on the way to a meeting, though nowadays you are very busy and have to get your assistant, Freeman, to do it for you.

One day, you are walking to an appointment when you realize you have left your watch at home. You need to know the time precisely. What do you do?

1. Ask someone.
2. Offer someone cash to tell you the time.
3. Ring Freeman and get him to make a take-over bid for a small clock-making firm in Switzerland, then ascertain the time from your new purchase and ring you back.
4. Use a nearby cashpoint to get some cash, knowing the time is printed on the receipt, and throw the money away.

You opt for the cashpoint and although the receipt duly tells you that it is 11.23 am, there is other, perhaps more interesting, news on the slip of paper. You are broke. Yes, there are no funds to cover your paltry request for £100. This is lunatic: you know for certain there is £50,000 in that account to cover your day-to-day expenses. And yet the computer says you are broke. What do you do next?

1. Laugh.
2. Cry.
3. Panic.
4. Fire someone.

You fire someone, of course – that's always a tycoon's first reaction in a crisis, to show that the blame lies elsewhere. So you go into a phone box at 11.26 am and ring Freeman to give him the bullet. To your amazement a voice says: 'Conrod Holdings here – can I help you?' With your financial experience, what do you immediately assume?

1. Your empire has been taken over by Conrod while you were out, Freeman is on the dole and you are about to be.

2. Freeman has formed a new company called Conrod in your absence and taken you to the cleaners.

3. You have phoned Conrod without thinking, because you are having a passionate affair with a woman who works there. (She arranges the flowers.)

4. You have a wrong number.

'Sorry, wrong number,' you say and hang up. You dial again and get straight through to Freeman. You're about to dismiss him, when he cuts you short.

'It's absolutely urgent, sir,' he says. 'We've just had a threat against your life. The police are taking it very seriously. We had to get in touch with you immediately, so as I knew you'd have to withdraw some cash soon, I took the liberty of closing your account temporarily. I knew that you'd ring me to fire me.'

Ingenious, you have to admit. But what's all this about a threat on your life? Who do you assume is after you?

1. Your wife.

2. The Monopolies Commission.

3. The husband of the girl who does the flowers at Conrod.

4. Almost anyone you've double-crossed on your way up, and that could be almost anyone. The threat, however, is anonymous. Freeman then tells you the address of a safe haven where you are to be within half an hour. (It is now 11.36.)

At 12.06, in fear and trembling, you ring at the bell of the address given and Freeman lets you in. Nobody else is there. You ask about the police. Freeman gives you a funny look and says: 'The police don't know about this, sir. You see, the death threat came from – me!'

It turns out that Freeman is the son of the chauffeur who died on the way to Exeter. He is convinced that *you* were doing the driving, and caused the crash, thus killing his father. You decide, as he raises his gun, to tell the truth as follows.

1. 'Yes, I was driving. Your father was a drunkard and I was looking after him!'

2. 'I was not in that car. It was stolen by your father!'

3. 'Your father never died in the crash! It was staged to allow him to start a new life in Brazil, after he had accidentally run a man over!'

4. 'The man who died in that crash was Wesley Brockbank! His identity was taken over by the chauffeur! Yes, son, I am your father!'

However, Freeman believes none of your explanations and raises his gun again. Pulling the trigger, he – oh, sorry, I've run out of space. You're on your own now.

That Which We Call a . . . What?

ONE of the things that makes complaining hard these days is not knowing what to call the thing you are complaining about. For instance, the sticky tape machine used by butchers, greengrocers and fishmongers to fasten bags. They pass the neck of the white plastic bag containing your purchase through the gadget and, hey presto! – it is efficiently sealed by an all-around piece of red or blue tape.

Once home, you pull it open and, hey presto! – nothing happens. The bag is sealed against you as well as against the environment.

If you are a novice, you then try to unpeel the tape carefully by hand. If you're a veteran, you have a pair of scissors or a knife to hand. If you're like me, ex-novice but untrained, you are reduced to wrenching the bag open with your bare hands and seeing the contents spill everywhere; not too bad if it is apples, less satisfactory if it is a pound of liver. You then leap up and down shouting, 'God, I really hate these . . .'

At this point you sink into frustrated silence because you don't know what to call them, and really haven't got the energy to jump around the kitchen shouting: 'God, I hate those little red and blue tapes which butchers and greengrocers use these days with those machines where you pass the neck of the bag – you know the ones I mean . . .' Instead, you take it out on some member of the family later, without either of you realizing why you're being so crabby.

Something else that gets my goat is the tiny plastic links that now join pairs of socks together. They also join labels to new trousers, and price tags to anything. They are so designed, like arrows or hooked barbs, that they are easy to get in but impossible to get out, which means if you try to pull your pairs of socks apart, one sock is going to rip. Maybe that's the idea . . .

Scene: The sock company boardroom
Chairman: Hoskins here has come up with a wonderful idea. Tell them about it, Hoskins.
Hoskins: Well, it's just that up to now we have joined our stocks together with a sticky label which only removes a few fibres when you pull if off. But if we were to link the socks with something that looked harmless but actually caused *real* damage to the socks, people would have to replace them. And that would mean them buying more of our socks.

Chairman: Tell them how you put it in.

Hoskins: You fire it in with a sort of gun. We'll encourage people to have these in shops, so they go around shooting at everything in sight – bit like police with plastic bullets, I suppose.

Chairman: No need to get controversial, Hoskins. Any questions?

Questioner: Yes. What are these ingenious and profitable things called?

Chairman: They're not called anything. Research shows that things without a name scarcely ever get complained about.

Of course, they've probably got trade names, but you and I don't know what to call them. I expect those heavy pieces of card that fall out of magazines on to the floor you've just swept have got professional names. 'Trade inserts', or 'boost sheets', or 'magazine flies', or something. But all you and I can say as the place is deluged with detached advertisements is 'Oh God, I wish they wouldn't put these bloody things, these you know, these free throwaway thingummies, oh, you know the things I mean . . .' By which time you've lost the attention of anyone who was listening to the beginning of the sentence.

Talking of tea bags, have you noticed how these days the posh ones have a label, or tag, or tiny paperback book, tied to them by string? Holding this very useful paper thing, you lower the bag into the mug, let go and pour in the boiling water. The force of the water pulls the string, and the paper object, into the mug, out of reach, and you moan: 'Godarnit, when I want to pull the bag out, I'll never be able to get hold of the . . . I wonder what it's called, incidentally?'

If you have successfully got a cup of tea (or at least a polystyrene beaker of dark fluid) in a public place, you will probably want to stir it, to amalgamate milk, sugar or artificial sweetener. You will look round for a spoon, but you will not find one.

What you find is a white plastic stick. The makers of spoons have decided that we no longer need to spoon anything like sugar (which now comes in a pourable sachet) and that the spoon bowl can be dispensed with. So we have instead a thing that looks like a white stick for a blind Action Man.

I don't like them much, I must say. I only wish I knew what they were called, so that I could say so.

How to Get by in Baby Language

WHEN my son was born, I took an oath never to write about him in print. Unless, that is, watching him had helped me formulate a major new theory about children which would be of help to all, or at least get me in line for a Nobel Prize for Child Watching. Well, today is such a day, as I think I may have stumbled across something which will help to explain children's behaviour more accurately than scientists have managed heretofore.

It's to do with the way babies learn to speak. My 16-month-old son has got to the stage where he can understand a lot of things we say, such as 'Put that cat down!' 'Turn that TV set off!' 'Do not eat that potted plant!' and 'I said, put that cat down!' but not say them back. This is understandable. A baby going round telling his parents to put the cat down and turn the TV off is clearly being taught the wrong phrases, and will become unpopular very soon. The sort of thing we should be teaching him, really, is, 'Thanks for the meal – it was great' 'I really like it here at home, you know' and 'Put the cost of all these toys and things on the slate, OK? I'll pay you back when I'm 21.'

But even if he cannot talk, he can speak. He makes a lot of different noises. Some of them are recognizable vowels and consonants such as 'Mumumum', 'Gagagaga' and 'Dududud'. Others are not recognizable: they are largely spitting, clicking, groaning, wheezing and fizzing noises which give him a lot of pleasure but are not going to be any use when it comes to learning English.

So we fond parents disregard the noises, but leap up and down when he goes: 'Bababababa', and say, 'Hey, he's trying to talk!' Actually, this is totally illogical. *He* doesn't know that Bababababa is going to be useful later on, and that the dribbling noises have no value in English. There are languages in which those noises *would* be useful. Xhosa is full of clicking noises, Afrikaners clear their throats a lot, Scots make noises that the English have lost and Poles makes sounds we never had.

All the noises he makes, in fact, are of possible use in some language. If he were a little African baby, his parents might be leaning over him every time he clicked and fizzed, saying: 'Ah, he's saying things already!' But if Bababababa and Gagagaga represented sounds they didn't use in their dialect, they would frown when he came out with them and wonder if he was ever going to learn to talk. There are sounds we all discourage our children from making, and if they

134

need them later on they are going to be in trouble.

We may think, for instance, that the Japanese have trouble with their 'L's and 'R's, but the British struggle with the French 'R'. Quite apart from the fact that the British think it's rather effeminate for a foreigner to talk French with a French accent, we actually find it very hard to wobble the saliva sufficiently in the throat to make the noise at all. We don't think it's a *real* noise, because it's not like any of *our* noises.

And yet children can manage it very easily. My son does it all the time, especially after fruit juice. And yet the odds are that I will get him to unlearn it before very long.

You see, what I think is happening is that the child, happily gifted with all possible noises, is busy listening to his parents to identify which language he has been born into prior to getting rid of the noises which he does not need. At the moment, he is poised to learn an African language or that branch of Chinese where they seem to be sick every other sentence, or even Japanese, but in six months the moment will be gone. Now is the time, or never, to get him talking fluent Yiddish, while he has the sounds for it.

But we shall, rather predictably, continue talking English in the home and his range of noises is about to be drastically pruned, not, as experts say, dramatically expanded. He may, through some freak, preserve a sound he doesn't need, or a consonant from some other language. I often wonder if the 'R' favoured by Roy Jenkins and Frank Muir or Tony Benn's whistling 'S' or that muffled 'S' peculiar to William Deedes, are not really authentic consonants from Ukrainian, or some cheap letter left over from a job-lot clearance of North African sound shifts. This may also explain why some children have trouble with one letter for years and years, getting all the rest perfectly right. The one they get wrong *is one they got rid of by mistake*, thinking it would not be needed in English. Maybe somebody in Afribzca got it by mistake and hung on to it, liking it.

Well, as I say, it is just a theory, but if the Nobel people are reading this, they know how to get hold of me.

'YOU know, Watson, I would be surprised if Lestrade were not the best travelled policeman in England,' said Holmes.

We were seated in the first class compartment of a GWR railway train, halfway through a journey which would bring us in another two hours to one of our great cathedral towns. My friend had received a telegraph from there reading: 'Holmes. Implore your help in case of missing bishop. Can see no daylight — Lestrade.' It is not like Holmes to refuse a challenge.

'He has certainly summoned us from some very diverse parts of England,' I agreed.

'I find his ubiquitousness instructive.'

'I fail to see how it can explain how a bishop vanishes while celebrating evensong, before the very eyes of the congregation?'

'Oh, pshaw!' cried Holmes. 'There's no mystery there. The affair is as plain as a pikestaff. No, what puzzles me is the regular way in which we are spirited to so many different locations, merely to clear up a murder.'

What Holmes says is true. We have found ourselves on lonely Yorkshire moors, along the wild Cornish coastline, in the depths of forests or in suburban railway tunnels. We have been called to stately homes and humble cottages. There is nowhere we have not been.

'Except the homes of the industrial poor, Watson, the places where they work and the roads they travel,' broke in Holmes. I nodded. Then I gasped, as I always do when Holmes completes one of my private thoughts out loud.

'Has it never occurred to you,' he continued regardless, 'that there is a certain similarity between the places we visit to find our mysterious murders?'

'Well, they certainly tend towards the bourgeois,' I agreed. 'Most of the houses have wistaria growing up the front, I have noticed. And the majority are within easy reach of a GWR line. Is that what you mean?'

'It is not at all what I mean,' said Holmes. 'I am referring to the considerable age of the houses. Their remote or self-contained surroundings. The wilderness of much of the country. They are all scenes which have not changed for many years, nor which are likely to change for many years.'

'I agree. But what . . .'

'Suppose, Watson, just suppose that our adventures together, which you have issued in book form, became so popular that they were presented on the stage. And just suppose that they remained popular for many years to come. And suppose furthermore that the infant art of cinematography were to become so expert that they could make the dramas of our stories into moving, talking pictures, which could perhaps be somehow brought into people's homes on a small screen . . .'

I truly believed my friend had gone mad.

'Well, Watson, things change so fast in this modern age that when they come to make these moving pictures in 100 years' time, they would find the whole scene totally altered. Horses would have been replaced by horseless carriages. Gas by electricity. Trains by flying machines. Brick buildings by this new concrete . . .'

'Yes,' I said, to humour him.

'Therefore it would make sense, would it not, to set our little stories in settings NOW which will change very little with time and which can be photographed a hundred years hence, in the 1980s, with no extra expense.'

'By Gad, Holmes!'

'This is what has happened already,' cried Holmes. 'We have already established that the scenes of our detection are all places untouched by the passing hand of man. The question we have to ask ourselves is: *Who is organizing this?* Who is arranging things now to make them convenient in a hundred years' time?'

'Why, Lestrade, I suppose,' I said, in jest.

'Exactly. I believe that Lestrade is in league with some moving photograph company *a hundred years from now*. I believe he summons us only to places which he can be filmed, as they call it, much later on. This cathedral we are going to now, for instance. Cathedrals do not change in 100 years. Nor does the way bishops dress. Oh, that, by the way is bound to be the explanation of the missing bishop. He went behind the altar and changed out of his robes. Nobody recognizes a bishop out of his robes.'

'But what are you going to do about the theory about Lestrade and his links with the future?'

'Quite simple. I am going to tax him with it and then suggest that we all three get a cut.'

But how this happened, and how we came to an agreement with a 'television' company not yet born, must form the subject of another story.

Burnt at the Stake,
or Your Money Back

'I HEAR they're having a medieval weekend over at Short Shrift village,' said Father.

'Oh, good,' said Mother. 'Will they be having archery, and jousting, and falconry?'

'Oh, yes, I jolly well imagine so,' said Father. 'And medieval music, and a bit of banqueting, and a whole ox, and perhaps an all-day mead bar.'

'But what if the children don't want to go?'

'What, Sylvia, Dick, Liz, Petra, Vivien, Wayne, Melvyn and the rest?'

Sylvia, their eldest, had been planned as an only child. All the other nine were accidental afterthoughts. It was not exactly what you might call a planned family, unless of course you were Catholic.

'Yes,' agreed Mother. 'They always seem a bit bored by this sort of traditional activity.'

'Well, children will be children,' said Father. A false idea, when you think about it. Children are children now – what they *will* be is something different and certainly not children.

But this time they were in for a surprise. Sylvia and Dick and all the rest were very keen to go to the medieval weekend. They said they had heard it was going to be good fun. Not one volunteered not to go.

'It certainly looks different,' said Father doubtfully, as they strode through the entrance come Saturday morning. Nowhere to be seen were the usual gay tents and proud flags that one associates with medieval times. Instead, there were a series of sad-looking wooden shacks, a man in the stocks whom people were bombarding with missiles, and what looked very like a gibbet with a body dangling from it. The children scarpered to have a look around.

'I find that in very bad taste,' said Mother, looking up at the dangling carcass.

'The Middle ages *were* in very bad taste,' said the corpse, much to Mother's surprise. 'That's the whole point we're trying to get across through this weekend.'

Father was about to ask who 'we' were when he was bundled out of the way by a couple of lepers rushing past, shouting 'Unclean, unclean!' Then Mother screamed. She was pointing at a full-scale rack, where two torturers were stretching a body on the diabolical instrument. The reason she was screaming was that the body belonged to her son Dick.

'Let him go!' she shouted. 'Let my son go at once!'

'Oh, for heaven's sake, Mother!' said Dick, looking up at her. 'It's only a *game*. I'm supposed to see how long I could have withstood medieval torture. It's really great. Oow!!'

Mother might have said something else except that just then an arrow thwanged into the building next to her, and she fainted.

When she came round, Father was beating off a First Aid helper who was trying to attach leeches to her.

'There's something very strange going on round here,' said Father grimly, 'and I intend to get to the bottom of it. Let's go and talk to the corpse again – he seems to know what's going on.'

'Hello, again. Having a good time?' said the corpse affably as it dangled aimlessly.

'Where,' said Father firmly, 'is the jousting, the archery, the falconry?'

'We don't have any of that sort of rubbish here,' said the corpse. 'Go to a theme park or an English Heritage function if you want a bit of plastic history, some pre-wrapped culture. We give you the real thing here.'

'AND WHO IS WE?' shouted Father.

'We are the Campaign For Real Heritage,' said the corpse. Just then a loudspeaker crackled and spoke.

'Good afternoon, ladies and gentlemen, and thank you for supporting the Campaign for Real Heritage in our fight against the heritage industry. Just to let you know that in a few minutes' time the Sealed Flask will be re-enacting the Black Death in the main arena. Half an hour after that, at 3.30, the Children's Crusade will depart for Jerusalem, and at 4 o'clock we will be ducking some of the mothers to see if they are witches. Meanwhile, look out for footpads, highwaymen, pick-pockets and low thieves who have all been trained at our Campaign for Real Heritage school. Thank you.'

Just then Dick and Wayne turned up, pulling excitedly at Mother's hands.

'Mum, mum, come quick, we've volunteered you to be drowned as a witch. Come on. And Sylvia and Liz are being tried for heresy. Come on!'

Despite himself, Father couldn't help smiling. It was the first time the children had ever displayed any interest in history.

(Would you like to know more about the campaign and help the fight against keg heritage? Write for details.)

139

Falling Asleep on the Motorway

IF I had to choose one book to take away on holiday, it would be:

Falling Asleep on the Motorway, perhaps the most important book to appear this year, being a study of the disease which we all suffer from but nobody ever dares mention. Like me, you must all know what it is like to get those prickly eyes and the intense feelings of inertia that precede an attack of motorway sleep. We have all known the terror of suddenly opening our eyes and finding we are heading for the back of a big French lorry, or, even worse, driving down the hard shoulder towards a parked AA van. We have all imagined that we were the only ones to suffer from it. That is why I urge you all to read:

Falling Asleep on the Motorway, the hilarious new novel by William Boyd, in which he follows the fate of an innocent Englishman abroad who dreams he is a member of a Dutch girls' hockey team. Embarrassed beyond measure because he does not know the Dutch for 'Where is the Gents', for God's sake?', he wakes up and finds he is actually driving down an enormous highway somewhere in America. He stops at a lonely diner to ask which state he is in, but when he finds opinion equally divided between Louisiana and Omaha, he comes out again only to find his car has been stolen. As a study of English manners abroad, there is no praise too high for:-

Falling Asleep on the Motorway, a volume of new poems by Brett Winkle, who has been described as the Tony Harrison of the Happy Eater. 'Coming from Watford, I espy/A lorry, well ablaze, near Leeds/With driver standing lonely by;/I am that man, my heart too bleeds.' This sense of empathy with the luckless lorry driver who had only nodded off for a second informs all Winkle's verse. Many of us have seen a truck standing pathetically with its cab bent down to the ground, as if broken-necked, but few of us have turned it into an image so constantly poignant as Brett Winkle's in:

Falling Asleep on the Motorway! A truly comical collection of celebrity tales about nodding off at the wheel, collected in aid of The Next Big Earthquake Fund. John Julius Norwich recounts deliciously how he keeps himself awake by reciting poetry, but once made the soporific mistake of reciting some late Wordsworth; Lord St John of Fawsley tells how Our Lady of Chelmsford came to him in a vision and stopped him hitting a bridge, while Spike Milligan tells a tale of running off the road in the Australian outback and not noticing till he got to Adelaide 1,000 miles later. There are countless similar heart-warming anecdotes in:

Falling Asleep on the Motorway, the screenplay of Dennis Potter's latest award-winning TV drama. It tells the sombre story of Jack Ambrose, a successful writer condemned to driving endlessly up to London and back for meetings about his latest play. Addicted to vintage popular music, he has an old 78 player installed in his car, but nods off during a particularly syrupy saxophone solo on a Rudy Vallee record and wakes up in hospital with steel needles and shellac fragments embedded all over him. Who can ever forget the moment when the surgeon tells him: 'I'm afraid you will always carry a piece of Bing Crosby's 'Some Of These Days' in your knee'? All this and more in:

Falling Asleep on the Motorway, Michael Heseltine's timely analysis of why Margaret Thatcher's economic revolution has begun to falter just when it should be reviving for the final push for the end of the motorway, which Heseltine makes the image of a thriving Britain. We have a little shut-eye only at our peril, is his message. Many of his ideas are thought-provoking; the suggestion of a glorious new garden festival in the Falkland Islands is not the least original suggestion in:

Falling Asleep on the Motorway, an informal history of Radio 3 Test match commentary from the earliest days. Many people who are not interested in farming are addicted to *The Archers* — similarly, many people who couldn't care less about cricket are self-confessed devotees of Brian Johnston and his merry crew. Indeed, Tom Stoppard, in a challenging essay, claims that there is no very great difference between *The Archers* and cricket commentary, though his notion that Brian Johnston and Bill Frindall are in some strange way a married couple is a little hard to swallow, as is his claim that Freddie Trueman has been played by three different actors over the years. But no radio cricket fan should be without his copy of:

Falling Asleep on the Motorway, the book for everyone on holiday. Get your copy now.

Orwell's 1992, Part One

Here is the first extract from a major new novel, George Orwell's 1992. Now that 1984 is out of date, we have computerized a fictional projection of the next really big year . . .

IT WAS a bright cold day and Winston Smith's watch was chiming 13. He must get it mended, he thought, but he knew he wouldn't; when you buy a watch for £1.99 from a service station, it's cheaper to buy a new one than pay for it to be mended. Not, he thought wryly to himself as he turned into the block where he lived, that he knew of any watch-mender to go to; they all seemed to have vanished these days.

Victory Mansions was a smart apartment block. Because of the recent bomb outrages, security at the entrance was very tight. Winston could not enter until he had spoken into the voice grille for speech identity, placed his hand on the print-plate for fingerprint identity and put his personal homecard into the slot provided. As if to make *sure* that he was not a dangerous terrorist, a television camera was angled towards him above the door and above that was a small hole which, Winston was convinced, contained the nozzle of a machine-gun. There was a rumour that a flat-owner in Maida Vale had been shot to death by a security device because he had mistakenly put a credit card in the homecard slot, but, like all such rumours, it had been hushed up.

The entrance hall to Victory Mansions was plush. This is a comfortable, spacious block, was the message it intended to convey, in which it lied, because the entrance hall was the only spacious and elegant room in the building. Accommodation was now so expensive in London that you were lucky to find anything bigger than one room for £250,000. On the other side of the partition wall Winston could hear his neighbour, Kimble, moving about. Sometimes, when it was very quiet, he could hear him breathing.

The lift door opened, and Kimble came out. He nodded at Winston without smiling.

'Off to Mincom?' said Winston. 'On a Saturday?'

'Something else blown up,' said Kimble. 'Have to go and deal with it.'

Primly he swept out of the building. What a prat, thought Winston. Ever since the new Secrets Act had come in, penalizing breaches of confidentiality, nobody who worked for the government ever talked about their job. This was a blessing in some ways, insofar as you were spared many a tedious conversation, but it also meant that nobody had any idea what the government was up to any more, unless they were in the know. Winston knew enough to remember that Mincom (the Ministry of Commerce) was the result of a merger of the old Department of Trade with the Foreign Office. Our Blessed Leader had decided the choice of our enemy should no longer not be left to diplomats, but was far better practised by businessmen.

It made sense, actually. History showed that the country which was your natural military enemy was often one of your biggest trading partners as well, which meant that wars could be costly business errors. When we went to war with Germany in 1914, we were attacking one of our biggest export markets. Not very clever. Fighting Argentina in 1982 had been much better, as Argentina was no great shakes as a trading partner; unfortunately, it had not been a military target either, and Winston privately though it had been a complete waste of time to fight a war 7,000 miles away.

It was the sort of thought that was best kept private these days. Our Blessed Leader repeatedly came on television to tell us how free we were, before announcing the withdrawal of another freedom. It was getting to the state where you could think whatever you liked, as long as it was more or less what the government thought.

As Winston let himself into his room, he could hear the telly droning on in the corner. It was Our Blessed Leader, live from Parliament.

'. . . therefore, in order to safeguard our precious freedoms, it is necessary that for a limited period only we withdraw the right of those arrested . . .'

It was quite extraordinary, thought Winston, how people swallowed the loss of freedoms when it was described as protection of freedom. A surge of hatred for Our Blessed Leader came over him and he reached for the remote control to switch her off. Then he remembered. It was broken. And there was no on/off switch on the telly. He was condemned to 24-hour television until he got it mended, with absolutely nothing else to listen to. In the distance there was an explosion.

'Except the bombs,' he thought, ironically.

Orwell's 1992, Part Two

The second extract from George Orwell's 1992:
Winston Smith couldn't turn his television set off because the remote control was broken and there were no knobs on the set. Consequently he was faced with a choice between Skytel, the entertainment channels, and Pubtel, or public service television. Skytel was non-stop, inane, screaming television conducted entirely by young people who laughed though no jokes had been made; Pubtel was extremely serious television conducted by grim people in half-lit studios who probably looked grim because they knew nobody was watching them. It was the same division as between the pop papers (Tabpress) and serious press (Qualpress), between serious music and Poprock . . .

It was very odd, thought Winston as he settled down to his evening Chicken *chasseur*. In all the science fiction he had ever read, from *Brave New World* onwards, governments had always forced mindlessness on the public to keep them quiet, had force-fed them rallies, cheap entertainment, quick thrills, non-think . . . But in 1992 people were *asking* for it. They demanded instantly forgettable music, bad papers and mindless television, thus doing the government's work for them. Every time 100,000 people turned up at Wembley to watch a Vidscreen of the singer on the stage (the singer himself was too small to see), the government could take a day off from pacifying the electorate.

Science fiction writers had also forecast that people would have space-age jargon forced on them, but that wasn't true either. They absolutely loved calling things Skytel, Pubtel, Poprock, Britgas, adspeak . . .

'Ow!' said Winston out loud. He had nicked himself slightly as he cut open the packet of what claimed to be Chicken *chasseur* before popping it into the microwave. Well, that wasn't quite true – most of the claims on the label were of what it wasn't and didn't contain. No salt, No butter, No cream, No fat, said one list. No salmonella, No brucellosis, No viruses, said another . . . This chicken has never eaten another chicken, said a third. The only reference to what it did contain came in the brief note: 'This packet contains only permitted ingredients'. The ingredients were not mentioned by name, presumably because it would breach some secret or other and some civil servant might incriminate himself.

This brought him face to face at last with the thought that he had been trying to evade all day, the memory of the conversation he had had with Kline at lunchtime. Winston Smith worked at what used to be called HM Customs and Excise but which was now renamed, in line with the trend, Vatex. They administered VAT, import duty, the new-fangled Travtax and more beside, but the department in which he and Kline worked ran the giant new customs area in Waterloo Station, due to be opened as soon as the Channel Tunnel was finished.

'How do *you* see 1992?' Kline said to him at lunch.

'It's a convenient way of separating 1991 and 1993,' said Winston. Kline was clever, but he didn't trust him. He would rather give him a flip answer than something Kline could turn against him. For once, though, Kline seemed in earnest.

'1992 is the year of Free Europe. Barriers come down, things flow freely, Europe takes a giant step, all one big family, blah blah . . . am I right?'

He was right, all right. Lets make free Europe work! was the omnipresent slogan, and only a few people like Winston lamented the lack of the apostrophe in Lets.

'So why are we building an enormous customs area in Waterloo Station?'

'Sorry?'

'Why is Vatex building Dutyhouse at Waterloo?'

Winston had heard the question perfectly clearly first time. He just hadn't believed it. It was their job, that was why. One might as well ask a paper seller why he was selling papers.

'1992 is the year we break down barriers, yet here we are building a huge barrier and nobody says a word,' continued Kline.

'Well, Waterloo is about to become an international station, so obviously it has to have its passport clearance, its customs area . . .'

'Rubbish. The big stations in Paris are international stations, have been for years, but they don't have customs halls.'

Winston hated conversations like this, where the ground started moving under your feet.

As he toyed with his Chicken *chasseur*, Winston brought himself finally to think about what Kline had suggested next: that he and Winston should sabotage the whole Dutyhouse complex.

Orwell's 1992, Part Three

The third extract from George Orwell's 1992:

'Hallo, it's Winston Smith here,' he said looking into the service till mirror. 'Can I have £500 please?'

In the old days, you just inserted a card and commanded the machine to give you money. Now, after so much fraud, the till had to recognize your face *and* your voice before it would give you a sum even as measly as £500.

'Do you promise that you are against violence?' said the service till to Winston. 'If you are a civil servant, do you promise to observe your oath of confidentiality? Will you tell the police anything you know about the bombings?'

'Yes, yes, yes,' said Winston testily. He was becoming increasingly irked by the government's paranoia about security.

'Here is your £500,' said the till. 'Have a nice day. Put your money away safely and try to buy British.'

'Get stuffed,' said Winston, but very softly. You could never be sure what was picked up. He put his £500 note into his wallet and wondered what he would spent it on. A bottle of Scotch? A visit to the cinema? He did not feel excited by either, but then, as an employee of Vatex (the old Customs and Excise) he could not get very excited about buying anything. He knew that 98 per cent of almost anything you bought, especially Scotch, went in duty and tax.

It had been rather boring in Vatex until he had met Kline. They worked together on the new Vatex hall at Waterloo Station (the so-called Dutyhouse) which was to greet travellers from the Channel Tunnel. And Kline had pointed out to Winston that 1992 was the year of Free Europe! Of no barriers! Of the end of tariffs! So why was Vatex building a huge customs hall at Waterloo?

Kline had suggested that their duty was to subvert and sabotage the building of Dutyhouse. As good Europeans, he argued, they should fight against duty barriers. Winston agreed. It was just . . . Winston should have realized that the reason he distrusted the government was that it was so sure about everything, and he didn't like people who were so sure. He should have spotted that Kline too was very sure about everything.

He stopped to buy an evening paper. The Americans had shot down another unarmed airliner. Scientists now thought that yoghurt might be a major health hazard. The Duchess of York's fifth child was doing well. Winston sighed and wondered why he ever bought a newspaper, as there was no news in it.

'Hardly worth £2.50, is it?' said a voice at his elbow. It was Kimble, his next-flat neighbour. Normally Winston couldn't stand the sight of milk-and-water Kimble, but for once he felt glad to see someone who wasn't going to force his opinions down his throat. 'I sometimes wonder why we bother.'

Grumbling about the price of things, Winston suddenly realized, was the illusion of freedom. The government let you moan about the cost of housing, or cars, or newspapers to let you feel you had the freedom to complain. What nobody ever complained about was the lack of news in newspapers, and that was really the only thing worth complaining about. That, he supposed, was why he felt drawn to Kline; Kline might be saying dangerous things, but at least he was providing an independent view. He was news.

As he turned into his road, there was a distant explosion. Another bomb. In 1992, when Europe was one big community, you were never quite sure whose bomb it was, because the Basques now set theirs off all over the place, and the Irish likewise. He let himself into his flat; it was only as he closed his door behind him that he realized there were two people there already.

'Mr Smith?' said one politely. 'Mr Winston Smith of Vatex?'

'The bastard who wants to sabotage all the computers at Waterloo?' said the other. Winston went cold.

'I don't know what you're talking about.'

They both wore suits and had very hard eyes. 'We've had some information about you from a good friend of yours.'

'Unlikely,' said Winston, 'I don't have any good friends.'

'That's not a very nice thing to say,' said a new voice. Winston turned. It was Kline, standing in a corner where he hadn't noticed him.

'Kline! *You* shopped me. But *why* . . .'

'Because you were bored, and therefore dangerous,' said Kline, 'and because you were about to discover the truth about Russia applying to join the Common Market.'

Orwell's 1992, Part Four

Fourth and final extract from George Orwell's 1992:

By 1992 a great proportion of the population could not remember a time when the country had not been run by Our Blessed Leader. Her voice, low and measured, covered the country like a layer of protective cloud. Winston Smith felt it sounded like one of those machines which quizzed you at bank service tills, quite comprehensible but with no feeling of life behind it. He dimly remembered having heard her on an old radio recording, and he knew that the way she sounded was due to the improvement she had undergone at the hands of the best sound coaches in the land. You couldn't help admiring a woman who had restructured herself in the way she had also restructured the country.

She had done the same with their enemies, come to that. In his youth, Winston could remember being taught that the great enemies of the country were Russia and China, and our great friends were America and Australia. Then Europe had become our friend, and Australia had started to fade as an ally, being taken over by America, which had also adopted China as a friend. It was all very confusing, so the country had turned to Our Blessed Leader for advice, and she had said quite unmistakably that Russia was the enemy.

Now, in 1992, she was saying that Russia was our friend, and everyone believed her. Winston almost believed her himself; but deep down he knew that something was badly wrong. That was no doubt why he had been picked up by the Secret Police.

'You're a hopeless case, Smith,' said his interrogator. 'Why can't you just accept things as they are, instead of probing behind the scenes?'

'Well, I just don't understand why in 1992, the so-called year of Free Europe, I should be helping to build an enormous customs and duty building in Waterloo Station. Why are we putting up barriers when everyone else is taking them down?'

'I will tell you why,' said the interrogator slowly, 'even though it is a waste of time. Now, who is our enemy?'

'It used to be Russia, but now we don't really have one.'

'Why Russia?'

'Because America hated Russia and we went along with the Americans. But there isn't so much tension between them any more, thank goodness.'

'You think it is a good thing to have friendship between Russians and Americans?' asked the interrogator, though it wasn't really a question. 'But for 50 years the enmity between Russia and America has produced world peace! Now, there is a big danger that America and Russia will become too friendly – Our Blessed Leader believes that if America and Russia become allies, they will unite against Europe. Against the EC. Against us!'

'How can you stop it?'

'By getting Russia to join the Common Market,' said the interrogator softly. 'By seeing America as the enemy, if necessary. Our Blessed Leader has a vision in which all Europe is united, under the morale leadership of herself and the Great Russian leader. Until then, she is trying to stop Western Europe from being too united. Hence her speeches against European federalism.'

'And hence the customs barriers at Waterloo?'

'Exactly. Of course, it is vital that no word of this ever gets out. That is why we must now send you to Room 625 . . .'

Room 625 was the place of ultimate torture. It was the room where they made you watch the television programme you most hated until you broke down. Winston most hated a consumer programme on which a toothy woman, who seemed like a strange parody of Our Blessed Leader, alternated incessantly between extreme sincerity and vulgar sexual innuendo. She was fawned upon by a succession of young men, rather as Our Blessed Leader was said to be treated by her Cabinet. Normally, Winston could only watch five minutes.

After 10 days, Winston was a broken man. Actually, he had been broken from the second day on, but they wanted to make quite sure. When he went back to work, nobody was keener on installing the customs hall than he. And when they tore it down again in 1998 to celebrate the USSR's admission to the EC, nobody was keener than he to get rid of it. Our Blessed Leader appeared with the Great Russian Leader to announce the formation of Great Europe, and to warn against the hostile manoeuvrings of the America/Japan/China axis.

Winston thought for a moment that he had known this was going to happen a long long time ago, but dismissed the idea as foolish, and went on cheering till he was blinded by tears of loyalty.

Your Irretrievable Breakdown Service

YES, of course you can create untold energy by simple nuclear processes at room temperature. I have been conducting experiments for upwards of 20 years using only a room, a thermometer and a nuclear family. The results are so staggering that I have never dared publish my findings. I only do so now because other scientists are rushing in with fraudulent claims.

Here is a small illustration of domestic energy creation. One member of the nuclear family gets up from the breakfast table in a kitchen at room temperature. He leaves behind a mug of black coffee, two-thirds finished, knowing that in a moment, after he has brushed his teeth or whatever he has gone to do, he will have a delicious slurp to come back to before leaving the house. He comes back. The mug has gone. Another member of the nuclear family has just washed it up. A spontaneous generation of energy then takes place, with the following exchanges of heat:

'Where's my coffee?'
'You'd finished it'
'No, I hadn't.'
'It had gone cold.'
'I like it cold.'
'It looked like washing up.'
'Well, in future, just leave ALL mugs of coffee.'
'In future, how would you like to do the washing up yourself?'

You see how in 15 seconds the discussion of one mug has ignited to create heat treatment of the whole relationship. The heat will simmer all day long, even when the two are apart, and the flare factor can be resumed at a moment's notice in the evening.

The formula for producing untold amounts of surplus heat and energy in the crucible of a nuclear family is $E = T \times t$, where E is for energy, T is for tension and t is for time. Scientists may point out that, although there was plenty of tension, there was very little time between the disappearance of the mug and the creation of the energy. But time in the equation includes *all* the previous times on which the mug has disappeared, and the time spent brooding over it. Here's another example of physical heat exchange:

'Don't.'
'Sorry?'
'Don't do that.'
'Don't do what?'

'What you're doing.'

'But I'm only listening to Mozart.'

'Isn't it possible to listen to Mozart without clicking your teeth?'

'I'm not clicking my teeth.'

'For 20 years you have been listening to classical music and clicking your teeth in time to it, and it's driving me crazy.'

'Then why didn't you mention it before?'

'I thought you would either stop or go off Mozart.'

And so on. You see, the time factor involved is 20 years, not the length of a Mozart concerto. That's why honeymoon couples don't get annoyed with each other and don't create energy; the tension is there, but not the time, as follows:

'What's that noise, darling?'

'It's Mozart, darling.'

'I know that, darling, I mean that clicking noise.'

'Oh, sorry, could you hear that? I'm afraid I have this habit or accompanying Mozart on my teeth.'

'You are *clever*, darling – you seem to know all Mozart. And I had no idea you could play the teeth.'

Not only sickening, but quite useless for producing energy. Still, just give them time. I said, incidentally, that a thermometer was used in my experiments. This was not used for measuring heat, only for being lost and thus creating more energy. As, for example:

'I've been looking everywhere for the thermometer.'

'Did you find it?'

'I wouldn't mention it if I had. Where have you put it?'

'What makes you think I've put it anywhere?'

'You're the one who always uses it.'

'Have you looked in the bathroom cupboard?'

'Yes – and that's another thing. It's a tip in there. So many out-of-date pills and tablets.'

'My fault, I suppose.'

'Well, you're the only one who uses these quack medicines.'

Have you noticed that the conversation has already left thermometers far behind? That's because it wasn't really a conversation about thermometers at all.

Here's another formula. $E = S \times d$. E is energy, of course; S is subtext, and d is the distance between the apparent subject of the conversation and the subtext, or real subject. In my next lecture I shall be showing how the incredible energy created in the average nuclear family actually blows it apart and causes irrevocable fission, at which point four or five missing thermometers inevitably turn up.

And He's Showing Him the ID Card

CAN you explain the purpose of this new football ID card scheme?

It's to help identify people in football.

What sort of people in football?

Well, players, mostly.

Are players hard to identify?

Yes, my goodness. Modern footballers are getting harder and harder to tell apart – they tend to play the same way, look the same way, go to the same hair stylist and all be called Kevin or Gary. They may also have Crown Paints and JCB Earthmovers written on their chest, although these are not their names.

Why not?

Because Kevin Crown-Paints would be a pretty stupid sort of a name.

But who would want to tell footballers apart?

Referees especially. Say, for instance, that a referee was peacefully taking charge of a game when all of a sudden he came across a footballer lying there unconscious. He's obviously been involved in an accident – stunned by a hit-and-run full-back, perhaps, or left for dead after an off-the-ball incident – so the referee has to identify him.

What about the number on his back?

I don't think that stands up in law, actually. I mean, you can't say on report form: 'The victim, who was numbered 19 and appeared to be called Crown Paints, had suffered multiple bruising etc . . .'

I suppose not.

But now the referee will be able to look at the recumbent man's ID card, get his name and address and then fill in a report.

And leave him lying there?

Oh, yes. Rule number one: never move the patient after an accident.

Who else is this ID card scheme aimed at?

Football managers.

Are they hard to tell apart?

Impossible, especially on TV. They stand around after matches wearing natty brown hats and using Identikit phrases like 'at the end of the day', 'we got a result', 'our tails are up now' and 'the season is far from over yet'. That is why they are introducing large-format lapel ID badges for managers.

How will that help?

As soon as the bloke appears with his big smile, saying: 'Well, it was a hard match, Brian, but we expected that and I think the boys played the game of their lives and I'm very proud . . .', the viewer can now, instead of saying: 'Who's this berk in the trilby?', actually lean forward and read his name and club.

Why do they all look so cheerful?

Because they only interview managers whose teams have won.

What happens to managers who lose?

They are unavailable. They have locked themselves in the changing room with their players for the talking-to of a lifetime.

Does that take a long time?

Yes. The players are all naked, so the manager finds it even harder than usual to tell them apart. That's why it will be so useful when they wear ID badges in the showers.

How do you attach an ID card to a footballer with no clothes on?

We are still working on that.

What about football chairmen? Will they have to wear ID badges too?

Oh, yes. That air of balding self-satisfaction makes them very hard to tell apart. And when one comes on TV and says: 'My board has 100 per cent confidence in the manager and we are behind him all the way,' it's very important that the manager in question should be able to identify him.

Why?

Because he is about to be given the sack by him.

Will football spectators also have to have ID cards?

It would be unfair if they were exempted from this, so yes, they will have cards too. There won't be any practical advantages in this, except that on big occasions it will serve to exclude ignorant outsiders who have just come along for a bit of a thrill and who tend to spoil the occasion for the real fans.

What sort of outsiders are you thinking of?

Members of the Royal Family. The Prime Minister. Politicians. People from Crown Paints, even.

There is a rumour that the government want to stamp out coin-throwing by crowds at players they don't like. Any truth in this?

Mrs Thatcher is certainly furious about coin-throwing but it has nothing to do with football violence. She sees it as part of the black economy, a completely untaxed transfer of cash from public to player. In future, anyone throwing coins at a player *must* get a receipt for it, and exchange ID numbers.

Thank you.

Not at all. Thank you.

A Really Useful Prince

THE ignorance of the media is sometimes quite frightening. When Prince Edward announced his intention to join Andrew Lloyd Webber's company, everyone said that this was the first big connection of royalty with the theatre. Have none of them read Shakespeare's plays, then? How could any of his histories have been written without a full cast of royalty to supply the subject matter? Plays, for instance, like:

Prince Edward, Part One
The scene is a theatre, full of actors, producers, backers and other riff-raff. Enter to them Keyhole, a press photographer.
Keyhole: What ho! Is this the place where shortly comes
Edward, Prince of Fleet Street, to start work?
Is this the noble house where, every night,
The hordes do come in charabancs from Kent
To gape at cats, or men on roller skates
Pretending to be trains, and swelling thus
The bulging coffers of the rich King Andrew?
Actor: Yes, ducky, 'tis.
Keyhole: Then here shall I straightway
Conceal myself till comes the Prince and then
Leap out to take a world exclusive pic!
Actor: Oh no, you won't. We've orders from the boss
To give all unknown folk like you
The order of the boot. The bum's rush. Out!
Keyhole: Here's a bank note of the realm, and all for you.
Actor: Ooh, that's a big one! You can stay! Hide here.
Keyhole goes into hiding as Prince Edward enters, disguised as a theatre person. He is accompanied by a personal detective, Sunshine, who is disguised as a personal detective.
Edward: At last! My true and precious home, the theatre,
Where I can be myself, not play at soldiers,
Nor imitate the prince or ape the scholar.
What say you, Sunshine? Is not the play the thing?
Sunshine: My lord, I very seldom go to plays.
The telly's more my line. *Allo, Allo,*
Is what I call a cunning piece of work,
So fairly wrought, yet saucy with it too.
Edward: Oh Sunshine, Sunshine, you are quite a one!

154

No, no, the telly's drab and dull. The theatre
Is the place! Here let me smell the paint,
Here let me put on robes and play the lord,
Or stand behind the scenes and tell the actors: Go,
Do this, Act thus, and Take it from the top.
Sunshine: You may be right, my Lord, and yet again you may be . . .
Edward: May be what?
Sunshine: . . . be wrong.
All this, the dressing up, the playing parts,
The telling some to come and some to go,
The acting out of grand and lordly roles
All this you do already as a prince.
Not well. But do it you most certainly do.
Edward: By right of birth alone, but not by merit!
To be the Queen's fourth child requires no art
Save that of shaking hands and showering smiles.
To be a real prince is nothing. But to pretend
To be a prince is something great and rare!
To be a player king and not a king!
Sunshine: That one's a bit too deep for me, my lord.
Edward: And thus I make my stand, to put off rank
And start from scratch, the lowest of the low
I'll be anonymous and in disguise,
With talent as my only guide and weapon.
Sunshine: Well, good luck, squire. You'll need it, by my troth.
Edward: But here comes one who has the thespian look.
Let's stop him now and ask where I'm to work.
Enter again the actor.
Actor: Hello, hello! Two strangers in our midst,
One tall and stocky like a constable,
The other young and fair. I like him best.
Perhaps my lucky day has come at last!
Sunshine: How dare you, churl? Know you not who he is?
Actor: Ooh, hark to macho man! 'Tis plain to see
This morn you left the wrong side of the bed.
Edward: Sunshine, quiet! . . . Pay him no heed, good friend,
But tell me where I now should go to work,
Which I must start today.
My name is Eddie Windsor.

*Trumpets. Fanfares. Great music. Enter to them Andrew Lloyd
Webber, King of Musicland and Lord of New York.*

155

Prince Edward, Part Two!

Story so far. Edward, a prince, has joined a theatre company in disguise as Eddie Windsor. Accompanied only by a private detective, Sunshine, he turns up for his first day at work, unaware that a press photographer, called Keyhole, lies in hiding for him.

As he is talking to an actor, a fanfare sounds for the arrival of a monarch. Enter King Andrew, with my Lord Palladium.

Actor: But here he comes, King Andrew of New York,
Crown Prince Lloyd Webber, Duke of Shaftesbury Ave,
Lord Argentina, Viscount Requiem . . .

Andrew: My Lord Palladium, what news has come?

Pall: Of what, great sire?

Andrew: Of what? The dollar, fool!
Each time the dollar sinks, I stand to lose
A million pounds in New York ticket sales,
And thou standst there and askst me, news of what?

Pall: Ah yes, the mighty buck. At dawn 'twas firm,
Then sank a little, but is up again,
Like to a moon which knows not when is day
And when is night, but wanders through the stars,
A pale, sick shadow of that sun, the yen . . .

Andrew: Do not call us, Palladium, we'll call you!
Go easy on the poetry; instead,
Inform us what new shows do ope today.

Pall: Your shows go on in 10 new towns tonight . . .

Andrew: Oh, pretty news!

Pall: . . . and close in five!

Andrew: Oh damn! Have you reviews to show me from the Press?

Pall: I have.

Andrew: Then burn them all. They like me not.
The English cannot stand to see success.

Edward: 'Tis strange to hear the way King Andrew talks.

Actor: So flat, you mean, and with a funny drone?
I think that all Lloyd Webbers talk like that.

Edward: No, no. His talk, I meant, is all of sales,
And contract work and copyright and cash,
And not of words or songs, as artists talk.

Actor: Oh deary me, you've got a lot to learn.

Andrew: . . . And no more cello pieces, tell my brother.

Pall: My Lord, 'tis done.

Andrew: But hold, who have we here?

Two knaves who stand and are not Really Useful?

Tell me your name, young man.

Edward: 'Tis Edward Windsor.

I start to work for you today.

Andrew: As what?

Edward: Why, marry, as production assistant.

Andrew: And know you what is done by a PA?

Edward: He is a lowly sort, my lord, who runs about,

Soothing actors' egos, doing the donkey work,

Learning the ropes, and then, in three months' time,

Shooting to the top.

Andrew: Oh, that will be the day.

Take this young man away and let him scan

The progress of my shares in Tokyo.

Sunshine: Hold hard. Stay there. Let no one move a thew.

Young Eddie stays with me, and I with him.

Andrew: Oh, does he now? And who are you to say

What happens in a Really Useful theatre?

Sunshine: I am a sort of guardian angel,

Whose task it is to keep this boy from harm.

Give me no aggro, and I'll give you none.

Andrew: I like this man! He wears a winning style

Which hath a certain stardom writ in it.

Dost thou not think, Palladium, that his voice

Rings charismatically across the stage?

Pall: I do, my Lord.

Andrew: Say, fellow, can you sing?

Sunshine: No, not at all, I fear.

Andrew: Who cares? Not I.

Full many a star of mine could hardly sing.

Come, fellow, stay with me and boldly shout:

'I'll be a star before the year is out!'

Exeunt all save Prince Edward and the actor.

Edward: The way ahead seems rougher now, by far;

While I am naught, my minder is a star!

Actor: The thespian's life is not a bed of roses;

More like a bed of well-manured neuroses.

It could be worse; at least you've got a job . . .

I don't suppose you'd lend me 30 bob?

Exeunt Edward and actor. Keyhole appears from hiding.
Keyhole: A scoop! A scoop! I see the headline now!
'Prince Edward blows it all again — and how!'
Exit, looking for a telephone.
CURTAIN.

A Foaming Mug of Wordsworth

THE Lake District has become the first National Park to acquire business sponsorship for one of its services. If you phone Windermere 5151, apparently, you get a fell-walking weather forecast 'in association with Cadbury's Chocolate Break'.

I'm all in favour of this sort of breakthrough, and I have been looking into ways in which it could be extended. I was just toying with the idea of having St Bernard dogs roaming the Lakes, vacuum flasks of Chocolate Break round their necks, and wondering what Wordsworth would think of it all when suddenly it came to me — sponsored Wordsworth!

It was the work of but a moment to run a favourite poem through the computer, together with the details of the sponsor, and this was the fascinating result:

> I wandered lonely as a cloud
> That floats on high o'er vale and hill
> When all at once I saw a crowd
> Of ramblers coming o'er the rill
> With multi-coloured anoraks
> And bulging rucksacks on their backs.
>
> Continuous as the cars that queue
> From dawn to dusk on the M1
> They paused to venerate the view
> The hurried onwards in the sun
> Looking for a place to take
> Their wouldn't-miss-it
> Chocolate Break.
>
> The waves beside them danced but they
> Did not quite trust the local water;
> Close to, it looked a little grey
> And not as healthy as it ought to.
> So each one brought a mineral flask
> Wherewith to carry out their task.
>
> They gathered wood, they lit the fire,
> And brewed their mugs of deep, rich brown.
> A poet could not but perspire
> When he had set the figures down

And worked out with a little thought,
What wealth to Cadbury this brought.

Now oft when, in my inward eye,
I see that Cadbury Choc Break packet,
I heave a plaintive little sigh
And wish that I could change my racket.
No more for me the poetry.
I want to work for Cadbury!

Unusual but invigorating, I think you'll agree. Encouraged by this, I tried feeding in that familiar first verse:

She dwelt among the untrodden ways
Beside the springs of Dove
A maid whom there were none to praise
And very few to love.

The computer soon gave me this sequel back.

And yet she did not seem to mind
Her rural solitude;
Great calm and peace she'd always find
When Chocolate Break was brewed.

'It is,' she said, 'a great mistake
With men your troth to plight.
All I need is a Cadbury break,
Brewed hot, last thing at night.'

She poured the powder in the cup,
Then milk, and gave a stir;
And when she took a little sup
Oh, the difference to her!

The one bit of Wordsworth I *had* to programme, of course, was all about your heart leaping up when you behold a rainbow ahead, meaning tolerable good weather for climbing and rambling, etc. Funnily enough, this is where the computer came unstuck. It couldn't really understand about bits of the body leaping up. The first attempt I got from it was:

My eyes leap up when I behold
A steaming mug of cocoa.
So was it when, a tender lad,
I thought all other drinks were bad,
So is it now I'm very old
And un poco loco.

I tried again.

> My ear leaps up when I discern
> The chink of spoon on cup.
> So was it when I first heard Mum
> Yell: 'Come and get your Choc
> Break, chum!'
> So is it now I've had a turn
> And can't get up.

I tried one more time.

> My nose leaps up when I locate
> That Cadbury Chocolate scent.
> So was it when, a little child,
> The smell of chocolate drove me wild,
> So is it now I'm eighty-eight
> And incontinent.

I gave up then, and went on to the last three lines: you know, all about the child being father of the man. This really stumped the computer, as well it might. Finally, I got this:

> The child is father to the man.
> Can this well be? Well, if it can,
> Then I'm the son of Desperate Dan
> And you're a squashed banana.

There's only one thing to do when a computer starts getting childish. Give up and send it to bed early.

The Roaring Forties

MORE today from the newly discovered Savoy opera, Trial by Forte, *which tells the improbable story of how Lord Forte sets his heart on wresting the Savoy Hotel, the only eating place in Britain he doesn't own, from Sir Hugh Wontner.*

ACT TWO SCENE ONE

The Savoy Hotel at tea-time. Enter an American couple, who are greeted by the waiter.

Waiter: You have booked a table for tea, madam?

Wife: Why, yes – we put our names down for it when we were last here in 1963.

Waiter: Alas, madam, the price of tea has now gone up to £25, but for that money you get a pot of tea, cake and biscuits, and a Savoy Hotel voting B share.

Wife: How very kind!

Waiter: Not at all, madam. As Sir Hugh Wontner always says: 'Beauty lies in the eyes of the B shareholder.'

Wife: How quaint! What does it mean?

Waiter: I have no idea. I thought it rude to inquire.

At that moment a large group of men rise from their tables and prepare to leave. They sing . . .

We eat and drink as much as we can
We stay till four and swill
But when they ask us for our cash,
We say: Put it on the bill!
We drink the best champagne on ice,
We only eat salmon and crab,
And when they mention settlement,
We shout: Put it on the tab!
You'll find us here at the Savoy
Imbibing till we're sick
But no one ticks us off at all,
As we get everything on tick!

They leave, shouting for taxis.

Wife: My good heavens, who were they?

Waiter: Lawyers, madam, working on the Savoy take-over bid. They

162

earn our money faster than they can spend it. Many of them see this case as a job for life. This way, please.

The Americans are seated, while Lord Forte and his son Rocco enter, disguised as members of the public.

Rocco: Must we come here to tea every day, father?

Forte: While they are giving away voting shares – yes!

Rocco: But why is it so vital for you to control the Savoy?

Forte: I just want somewhere of my own I can ask my friends back to. Is that so wicked?

Rocco: You have so many hotels already!

Forte: Pfah! My THF hotels are for English people, not people of discrimination. Look round here; how few English people you see, and how many foreigners with taste and finesse.

Rocco: And Americans.

Forte: Never criticize Americans. They have the best taste that money can buy.

Rocco: Then what is so wrong with English taste?

Forte: Listen, and I will tell you.

He sings . . .

> When I was young, the bottom rung
> Of the ladder to success
> Was learning how to serve up chow
> With minimum finesse.

Rocco: With minimum finesse?

Forte: Oh, yes. Or even less.

> The English do not like a stew
> With spices and what-not.
> They like it NOW, and they don't care how,
> So bring it quick and hot.
> You never never can hear an Englishman
> Complaining of the taste;
> You may be told, 'This dish is cold',
> Or even, 'Make more haste',
> But if a dish should taste of fish
> When he'd ordered Côte de Veau,
> He'll never cuss or make a fuss
> – He'll pay and quietly go.

Rocco: What, no resentment show?

163

Forte: An Englishman? Oh no.

> So when I was a lad, I always had
> My eye on English taste;
> A meal at a café, or a day at the Naafi,
> Was never a total waste.
> Throughout the Blitz, I watched the Brits
> Eat macaroni cheese,
> I watched them chew a sort of glue
> Which they called mushy peas;
> I watched them munch their way through lunch
> Then have the same again for tea.
> And I thought to myself, on the bottom shelf,
> It's a caterer's life for me!
> So I always gave them the food they crave,
> Which earned me piles of dosh.
> Don't call me rude, but the British HATE food;
> The thing they like is nosh!

Rocco: Not medaillons en broche?
Forte: No, chips and orange squash.
Rocco: And that's why you're rich and posh?
Forte: Yes, you could say that.
Rocco: Gosh.
Forte: Well, perhaps not posh yet, but as soon as I get enough Savoy shares . . .
Rocco: Look, here comes Sir Hugh Wontner.

[*Sir Hugh enters surrounded by cheering shareholders.*]

Sir Hugh: Drinks on the house! Magnums of fizz!
The cheering shareholders chair Sir Hugh off as Lord Forte and Rocco, temporarily defeated, scowl at their tea and gnash their sandwiches.

A Rose by Any Other Name, Like Stinkwort

FOR A long time now there has been a conspiracy of silence about first names. If you buy a book of names – whether to choose a reasonable one for your new baby or simply to find out if Sebastian actually means anything – you are given the impression that every name has a lovely meaning. Names in books always mean things like 'child of beauty' or 'messenger of grace'.

The truth is quite different, as anyone whose name has been laughed at will testify. Many names have ludicrous, even distasteful interpretations. *Yet no book has ever listed any of these meanings.*

Well, today represents something of a major and pretty courageous breakthrough, as I have prepared a small glossary of Names With Awkward or Unpleasant Meanings – a thing never before attempted.

If anyone is offended by inclusion on this list, I am sorry, but I spent far too much time at school being called 'Kilometres' to be soft-hearted about this.

Abie: Name with no meaning at all, chosen at random from two consecutive letters of the alphabet (cf Kael, Elim, Eno, Opie, Este, etc.).

Artie: The second worst insult in Britain, after intellectual.

Ben: Cold, stark, lump of stone at top of Scottish mountain (see Cliff).

Bent: Common Swedish forename (see Gay).

Bill: To demand money from (see Sue).

Bob: To go up and down aimlessly (see Eddy).

Charlie: A twit, a nincompoop, as in 'a proper Charlie' (see Dick).

Chris: A strong laxative, as in Swiss Kriss, which, as all jazz fans know, was Louis Armstrong's favourite medicine.

Clark: Lowest of all grades.

Cliff: Large amount of cold, inert material (See Rock).

Colin: French coarse white fish.

Derrick: A large lifting device (see Jack).

Di: To perish.

Dick: Slang male anatomical term; can also mean twit, as in 'a bit of a Dick' (see also Herbert).

Eddy: To go round and round in circles pointlessly (see also Bob).

Emmy: A vulgar, gaudy, showbiz ritual (USA: see also Oscar).

Eve: Girl's name which suddenly changes sex in mid-Channel and becomes Yves.

Fanny: Slang female anatomical term.

Frank: Bereft of tact.

Freddie: Cold (Italian).

Gay: see Bent.

Grace: A mumbled, incomprehensible bit of dog Latin which prevents diners from getting at their meal.

Guy: To make fun of.

Harry: To pester or constantly annoy.

Henry: A hooray Henry, a male Sloane.

Herb: A weed.

Herbert: A twit (see Norman).

Jack: Small lifting device (see Derrick); also knave.

Jake: Lavatory, usually in plural (see John).

Jean: Another name which inexplicably changes sex in middle-Channel.

John: Lavatory (see also Lew);

John Thomas: slang male anatomical term popularized by D H Lawrence.

Johnny: Contraceptive.

Kit: Luggage and baggage.

Les: Short for lesbian.

Lew, Lou: Lavatory, att: Dead, useless (German).

Nellie: Slang female anatomical term (as in 'Not on your Nellie').

Nick: The devil, also to steal (see Rob).

Norman: A twit, a buffoon (see Wally).

Oscar: Vulgar, gaudy, showbiz occasion (see Tony).

Pat: Cow's dropping.

Paul: To dwindle, dribble away (see also Peter).

Percy: Slang male anatomical term.

Peter: To dwindle, dribble away (see Wayne).

Rob: To steal or burgle (see Nick).

Rock: Small piece of inert material (see Ben and Cliff).

Roger: Unsocial activity, usually undertaken by lodgers.

Ron: Spanish for rum.

Sally: An attempt at a joke.

Sean: With the hair cut unpleasantly short.

Skip: A place to dump rubbish.

Sue: To take a person to court in an attempt to remove all his money.

Tom: An American black person who lets down his race by treating whites obsequiously (from Uncle Tom).

Tony: A vulgar, showbiz occasion.

Wally: Yet another word for a twit or nincompoop.

Wayne: Yet another word for to dwindle, dribble away (see Wilt).

Willie: Yet another slang male anatomical term.

Wilt: To feel suddenly weak with the effort of finding unpleasant names beginning with Y or Z.

Multiple Choice Conversation

IS IT my imagination or has there been a strange development in the way we talk in the 1980s? Have we all become multiple choice speakers? Here, for instance, is an exchange I sometimes hear in my local pub.

'Bitter, please.'

'Right – pint or half?'

'Half, please.'

'Best or ordinary?'

'Best, please.'

'Straight glass or handle?'

It's more like filling in a form than having a conversation. It happens in the buffet of my local station, too.

'Coffee, please.'

'Drink here or take away?'

'Take away, please.'

'Black or white?'

'Black, please.'

'Large or small?'

'Large, please.'

'Sugar or no sugar?'

And that's without the milk *vs* cream battle, the hot *vs* cold milk, or even brown *vs* white sugar controversy. The same quasi-bureaucratic process can take place when buying rail tickets, getting a glass of wine, booking a hotel room or even trying to get hold of a drink of water.

'Sparkling or still, sir?'

'Oh, sparkling, please.'

'A large or small bottle?'

'Small, please.'

'Ice and lemon, or plain?'

I seem to remember that when amoeba breed, they simply split into two and carry on. Our sentences are getting like that. Every statement can immediately be subdivided into two further possibilities. At a recent wedding, when the vicar asked the groom if he would take his bride for richer or for poorer, I am sure I heard the groom reply: 'For richer, please.'

You can always try to circumvent this self-perpetuating process by putting all the answers in your very first request. I have tried it.

It doesn't work. Here is a conversation I had at that local station buffet recently.

'A large black coffee to take away, please.'

'Right, sir . . . *Pause to find fresh supply of mugs under counter* . . . Sorry, was that black, sir?'

'Yes.'

'Right. Did you say large?'

'Yes, I did.'

And so on. You cannot win. I thought I had won last week when I said to the lad at the buffet: 'One black coffee. In a LARGE mug. No sugar. Repeat, black coffee in a large mug to TAKE AWAY, no sugar. All right?'

But he merely looked at me and said: 'Do you want the lid on or not?'

One of the reasons I gave up smoking was that I couldn't simply buy a packet of cigarettes any more. I had to undergo interrogation.

'Plain or filter?'

'Filter, please.'

'King-size or ordinary?'

'Ordinary.'

'Flip-top or standard pack?'

The thing that worries me about all this is the illusion it creates that we are getting more choice than ever before – that each question represents a true option for the customer, created by a loving producer. Almost the opposite is true. The more questions we are asked, the less likely we are to be offered any choice at all. My local station buffet offers one kind of coffee, and that's it. Whether the water comes sparkling or still, in a large or small bottle, it's the same water.

Even when the waiter asks you if your steak is to be well done or rare, you know in your heart of hearts that most British restaurants will do it medium well done, whatever you ask for. Even when the hotel asks you if you want a twin, double or single room, you know that every hotel today will give you a twin room even if you want a double or single; they will just charge you differently, that's all.

Even in my local pub, the publican's information-gathering technique (Half or pint? Straight or handle?) cannot disguise the fact that he sells only Courage's beers. It is not his fault. Courage, which owns the pub, will not let him sell any other kind of local beer unless he signs a different and much more hard-hearted agreement. It's a spurious choice, like buying sausages.

'A pound of sausages, please.'

'Pork or beef, sir?'

'Pork, please.'

'Ordinary or chipolatas?'

'Chips, please.'

'Herby or plain?'

But whatever the introduction, you are about to meet the same old bready, cereal-filled, flavourless British sausage. Because there are lots of questions, we fail to notice that there are only a few different answers. Multiple choice conversation is a conjuring trick in which the conjuror goes on about the size of the mug or chatters about the label in order to distract you from the central lack of choice. Which brings me to the American presidential election . . .

The Great All Day British Opera

ACT ONE, SCENE ONE *Enter a chorus of architects, heavily cloaked. They prowl around till they have made sure that the Prince of Wales is not nearby. Then they sing:*

In days of yore,
We'd have in store
The most palatial effects.
But now, in flocks,
We build large blocks
– We're British architects.
If a man pulls down
A nice old town
And a shopping mall erects,
He's not a vandal,
There's never a scandal
– We're British architects!

(What on earth is going on here? Well, dear reader, you must have read that the Royal Opera House is about to trample on the residents of Covent Garden by turning half the place into profit-making offices and shops, and car parks. I am busy turning the whole story into a new opera, to be called The Pirates of Covent Garden, *and these are tantalizing extracts.*

The architects creep away, attracted by the clinking of money off-stage, and Arnold enters. He is the champion of the residents, a handsome graphic designer who does not go home to Fulham at night but actually lives here! He sings an aria called 'La Piazza Mobile' along these lines:

I cannot sleep, for in the square
A monstrous screen is standing there
With forms that bawl, and
    rant and roar,
And shadowy shapes that cry,
    encore!

He is referring, of course, to the outdoors screen which inflicts opera on the residents from the time to time in order to subdue them, except on Sundays. I may introduce an aria here entitled 'Placido Domingo' (Peaceful Sunday), but I am not sure. Anyway, next on the scene is Amanda, who is in love with Arnold. Unfortunately, she is also the only daughter of the chief planning officer for Westminster, which creates a certain conflict of interest.

Arnold: Amanda! What are you doing here?

Amanda: My father has brought us to the opera, and I have slipped out during the interval to see you.

Arnold: But he will miss you!

Amanda: No, no. He always sleeps through opera. It is the only rest he gets. Poor man, he works so hard.

Arnold: Yes! Working to pull down Covent Garden! Drawing up plans for the destruction of our homes! So that we can have more car parks and offices and penthouse flats!

Enter, on cue, chorus of architects. They sing:

Our work's never done
In WC1
But our home's in Middlesex;
We'd never live here
Where we work – no fear!
We're British architects!
They slink off again.

Arnold: You see? They are monsters! They wish to convert our dear old Covent Garden into a concrete desert!

Amanda: Darling, why do you talk so loud, with so many exclamation marks?

Arnold: I don't know! Perhaps I too am in an opera! How terrible! To be in such an elitist art!

Enter the chorus of the Friends of Covent Garden. They waggle their fingers reprovingly at Arnold and sing, in hurt tones:

You mustn't think that we are snobs,
We modern breed of opera-goers,
We're Sues and Ritas, Bills and Bobs,
Not Elspeths, Loelias, Marks and Noahs!
We really have a jolly time
In the crush bar, ever so merry.
What's yours, Doris? A lager and lime?
I think I'll risk a little sherry!
They flounce off.

172

Arnold: You see? Opera used to be the preserve of the dreary old aristocracy. Now it is being taken over by the dreary petit bourgeoisie.

Amanda: Oh, but here comes my father! I must run!

Arnold: When shall I see you again?

Amanda: At the next inquiry!

She exits. Arnold exits, after singing the aria 'Have you booked your drinks for the interval? It really helps the staff . . .' In the distance we hear the chorus of architects singing:

Oh, some like drink
And some like to think
And some like plain old sex,
But our biggest treat
Is stained concrete
– We're British architects!

And the curtain falls. Well, that's just the first scene. If there is sufficient public interest, I will bring you the ensuing four and a half acts in instalments. The opera is to be in English with Italian sub-titles, and the rights will be auctioned sometime next month.

Is There Libel After Death?

LEGAL history is being made by a case in which a living man is being sued for a libel uttered after his death. How is this possible? Let us find out by studying this extract from the start of the trial on Monday.

Counsel: You are Gerald Fang?

Fang: I am.

Counsel: Are you dead?

Fang: No, I am alive.

Judge: Have you ever been dead?

Fang: Not to my knowledge.

Judge: This is an extraordinary line of questioning, Mr Garstang.

Counsel: Libel can only be committed by a living person, my Lord, so I have to establish if the defendant is alive.

Judge: I have presided over many libel cases before, and never as I recall was the defendant a dead person. Though occasionally the defence counsel showed very few signs of life. (*Laughter in court*) There, I have made my little joke, and now you can carry on as you like for a while.

Counsel: Thank you, my Lord. Mr Fang, I presume you have made your will.

Fang: I have.

Counsel: I believe you have made a video to be shown as the will is read.

Fang: Yes, I have. There will also be a short but very funny animated film from Hungary.

Counsel: Quite. Could you briefly describe your video?

Fang: It is a fast-moving, entertaining, slickly edited short film which shows considerable promise for a first production. How sad to learn that it is also this producer's last production.

Counsel: It is not a rave review I am after, Mr Fang, but a bald précis of the film.

Fang: It is a wave from beyond the grave. It is an on-the-spot report from Gerald Fang, River Styx, *News at Ten*.

Counsel: Death is no laughing matter, Mr Fang.

Fang: It is my death we are talking about. I can film myself saying goodbye and good riddance, can I not?

Counsel: Ah! Good riddance! An instructive phrase. Are you

174

suggesting, Mr Fang, that you make some comments in the film about those still alive? Have you taken the opportunity of uttering words of malice and contempt about those of your contemporaries whom you wish to wound from beyond the grave?

Fang: All right, yes, I have made a few barbed comments, but there isn't that much talking in the film. I mean, it's mostly archive film of my early life, sequences of me tap-dancing . . .

Judge: Tap-dancing, Mr Fang?

Fang: Yes, my Lord. I was a bit of a hoofer in my day, and I wanted to get it on film before I lost the knack.

Judge: I hope you do not sing 'My Way' on this video.

Fang: Certainly not, my Lord. Nor 'Send in the Clowns'.

Judge: Good. I come to this court to get away from television shows. Carry on.

Counsel: At any point in the film do you make comments about my client, and your business partner, Mr Victor Musket?

Fang: Yes, I do.

Counsel: Are they of such a nature as to suggest that Mr Musket is incompetent, fraudulent, evil-smelling, unreliable, unable to tap-dance and possessed of the most annoying laugh known to man?

Fang: I really can't remember. I made the film some time ago.

Judge: Mr Garstang, would it not be simpler to produce the film and see for ourselves?

Counsel: I do not have access to the video, my Lord.

Judge: You mean, you haven't seen it?

Counsel: No, my Lord.

Judge: Then how on earth do you or your client know there is any libel in the film?

Counsel: By a strange coincidence, the technician who worked on the film is related to Mr Musket's wife. He happened to mention the rough gist of what Mr Fang has said. It seemed highly libellous.

Judge: Then we must order this video film to be produced at once. Mr Fang, please arrange for this.

Fang: I cannot, my Lord.

Judge: And why not, pray?

Fang: My Lord, this film is designed to be seen after my death. It contains material which, if shown in my lifetime, could involve me in litigation.

Judge: It already has.

Fang: What I say about Victor Musket is quite mild compared to some of the other things I say about relatives and friends. If you order this film to be shown in court, then *you* will become the

175

instigator and accomplice of libellous statements of which the world yet knows nothing.

Judge: You claim that showing the only piece of evidence in this trial would make a criminal of me?

Fang: I certainly do.

Judge: This is quite unprecedented. The case is adjourned while I think about it.

The Wit and Wisdom of Albania

I AM working on an anthology of Albanian proverbs and sayings. The difference between Albanian proverbs and every other kind is simple. Most proverbs sound simple and turn out to be full of wisdom; Albanian proverbs sound as if they are making a deep comment on the human condition but mean nothing at all. I am printing a selection of them today to give you some idea of this little-known art form.

*

When you reach the top of a queue, do not feel happy; you are on the point of becoming the end of another queue.

*

In the country of the flip-flop, the shoe-shine boy eats poorly.

*

If a teapot and a lid do not match, is it the lid that does not fit the teapot or the teapot that does not fit the lid?

*

Humour is only said to be international because nobody can agree about it at home.

*

If a marriage can survive the honeymoon, it can survive anything.

*

A horseman feels faster and higher than the rest of mankind, but the best jockeys are the smallest and slowest men.

*

If all the foundation stones ever laid by all members of royal families were put together, who would want to live in the result?

*

Schoolfriends called 'Fatty' never reappear in one's adult life.

*

Famous people are said never to make real friends when they are famous, but always retain the friends of their youth. However, all the friends of our youth who are now famous never come to see us any more. How can this be explained?

*

Money is all very well, but it cannot buy riches.

*

The world is full of men who started out in life saying they would not under any circumstances accept a decoration from the Government, and then were never offered one.

*

Do not trust a cookery writer who has written books about more than three countries.

*

Who ever saw a statue erected to a sculptor?

*

When a man finds his admiration for his wife turning to irritation, he should be careful not to place a pedestal on her.

*

The only surviving legacy of the British Empire is the curious expectation among British people that all black people should naturally be able to speak English.

*

It is not the people who gave us gifts that we remember most, but the ones we failed to thank.

*

Dutch Elm Disease reached every country except Holland. Holland, on the other hand, is the only country where they had Belgian Elm Disease.

*

Why is it that honeymoon couples always book into a hotel one grade above their real social level?

*

The only special thing about a special relationship between two countries, such as America and Britain, is that nobody is aware of its existence except the weaker of the two countries.

*

There comes a state in every man's life when he no longer wears his medals and decorations; they begin to wear him.

*

If people who designed the shape and size of postcards had ever got together with people who design the shape and size of postage stamps, one of them would look very different.

*

What is it that all women have but no man ever does? A spare paper tissue. What is it that all women know but no man ever does? The birthday dates of their loved ones.

*

It would be worth being an honorary doctor if there such a thing as an honorary disease.

*

Concert-going: how can a man who demands nothing less than Beethoven to listen to, be content with the back of the conductor's head to look at?

*

An instant apology is guaranteed to offend.

*

All women finally come to look like their favourite possessions. A lower-class woman comes to resemble her handbag, a middle-class woman grows more like her pets and an upper-class woman comes to look like her late husband.

*

From The World's Greatest Albanian Sayings. Strictly Copyright.

FOR THE BEST IN PAPERBACKS, LOOK FOR THE 🐧

In every corner of the world, on every subject under the sun, Penguin represents quality and variety – the very best in publishing today.

For complete information about books available from Penguin – including Puffins, Penguin Classics and Arkana – and how to order them, write to us at the appropriate address below. Please note that for copyright reasons the selection of books varies from country to country.

In the United Kingdom: Please write to *Dept E.P., Penguin Books Ltd, Harmondsworth, Middlesex, UB7 0DA.*

If you have any difficulty in obtaining a title, please send your order with the correct money, plus ten per cent for postage and packaging, to *PO Box No 11, West Drayton, Middlesex*

In the United States: Please write to *Dept BA, Penguin, 299 Murray Hill Parkway, East Rutherford, New Jersey 07073*

In Canada: Please write to *Penguin Books Canada Ltd, 2801 John Street, Markham, Ontario L3R 1B4*

In Australia: Please write to the *Marketing Department, Penguin Books Australia Ltd, P.O. Box 257, Ringwood, Victoria 3134*

In New Zealand: Please write to the *Marketing Department, Penguin Books (NZ) Ltd, Private Bag, Takapuna, Auckland 9*

In India: Please write to *Penguin Overseas Ltd, 706 Eros Apartments, 56 Nehru Place, New Delhi, 110019*

In the Netherlands: Please write to *Penguin Books Netherlands B.V., Postbus 195, NL–1380AD Weesp*

In West Germany: Please write to *Penguin Books Ltd, Friedrichstrasse 10–12, D–6000 Frankfurt/Main 1*

In Spain: Please write to *Longman Penguin España, Calle San Nicolas 15, E–28013 Madrid*

In Italy: Please write to *Penguin Italia s.r.l., Via Como 4, I-20096 Pioltello (Milano)*

In France: Please write to *Penguin Books Ltd, 39 Rue de Montmorency, F-75003 Paris*

In Japan: Please write to *Longman Penguin Japan Co Ltd, Yamaguchi Building, 2–12–9 Kanda Jimbocho, Chiyoda-Ku, Tokyo 101*

MILES KINGTON

AROUND THE WORLD WITH EIGHTY TV TECHNICIANS

In 1990 Miles Kington set out to follow in the footsteps of Michael Palin on his intrepid journey around the world, in which the ex-Python attempted to keep sane in the company of an entire TV crew. As we now know, Michael Palin succeeded in his attempt to get round the world in less than 80 days, but failed to retain his sanity. Driven mad by requests to do it just one more time, take another take because there was a plane overhead, and above all to have supper in the company of a TV crew seventy-nine evenings in a row, Palin is now a wreck of his former self, reduced to signing copies of his bestselling book and smiling in public when asked: 'Off round the world again, then, Mike?'

Is it *possible* to go round the world with a film crew and retain any vestige of sanity? Does one have to be mad to agree in the first place? Why did Palin insist on getting a train across China when it would have been much quicker to get a boat from Hong Kong to Japan? Was he forced to do this by a producer who feared Palin was going too fast? Or was he bonkers by this time anyway? All these questions are answered in Kington's travel epic *Around The World With Eighty TV Technicians*, in which, for instance, he reveals that Palin opted for train across China in the expectation that nobody there would refer to him as 'ex-Python Palin'.

'And nobody did,' reports Kington. 'Unexpectedly, however, he was mistaken for Paul Theroux's younger brother and had to pay a lot of bills left unsettled by Theroux on his Great Railway Bazaar journey. What with ten years' interest accruing, this virtually wiped out Palin's advance on his BBC book. None of that appeared in the film, of course. The BBC censor almost everything these days.'

This is not the first time that someone has gone round the world with a TV crew. It is, however, the first time that anyone has done it and not made a film. It may never be done again. This is the story of how it happened.

GREAT MYSTERIES OF OUR TIME
– SOLVED!

Have you ever noticed that the pictures of authors on
the backs of books, or at the top of articles in magazines, always show someone ten or fifteen years
younger and much more good-looking than the author
really is? Have you ever wondered how this uncanny
phenomenon came to be?

In his new guide to great mysteries of our time,
Miles Kington provides the explanation at last.
What happens is this. The author writes the book,
or article. It is accepted. The author then hears no
more about it until, the day before it goes to press,
the picture department rings up. 'Oh, hello,' they say.
'Look, we need a black and white head and shoulders
of you, please, and could we have it in an hour's time
at the reception desk? Ta.'

'Why didn't you ask for it before?' says the author.

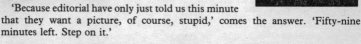

'Because editorial have only just told us this minute
that they want a picture, of course, stupid,' comes the answer. 'Fifty-nine
minutes left. Step on it.'

The author digs out one of the few current photos of him or herself, and sends
it round to the publishers. After this has happened a few times, the author has
run out of current pictures and starts digging into the family files, the holiday
albums, thus going further and further back in time. Those younger photos are
not caused by vanity, but by the total absence of anything more up-to-date.

'Another great mystery of our time,' says Kington, 'is why authors don't write
at the end of their manuscripts: "Ask the picture department *now* to come round
and take a picture of me". The answer is: Because they're stupid.'

MORE FORTHCOMING BOOKS BY

MILES KINGTON

to be published in Penguin

MORE GREAT MYSTERIES OF OUR TIME – SOLVED!

In his first volume of great mysteries of our time, Miles Kington explained such contemporary puzzles as how to brew your own Aqua Libra for 3p a bottle, why so many rich people let Alan Whicker into their homes and whether Norman Fowler did, in fact, get to spend any more time with his family.

'I've also answered that great question of our time: "Why has Mrs Thatcher never answered any question put to her?"' says Kington. 'The answer is, of course, that she was answering a series of questions which *hadn't* been put to her, and I have given a complete list of these, previously unpublished, questions. But I think my proudest achievement in this book is to tackle the question *everyone* has asked: "Why do people flash headlights at me when there is nothing wrong with my car?"'

It puzzled Kington for a long time, too. Till one day, when he was driving into Brighton and a car coming out of Brighton flashed its headlights at him, he began to see the answer.

'I automatically assumed that he was flashing me because my headlights were on. I turned my headlight switch. But then I suddenly realised that I had just turned my headlights *on*, and they had been off previously. I was about to shrug and think no more of it, when I also realised that I had flashed someone else on the far side by accident, a few cars back from the original flasher. Now, the car I had just flashed would think his headlights were on and would try them, and thus flash a car somewhere behind *me*, and so on.'

Kington realised with a flash of intuition that he was part of a great chain of cars all flashing each other at a few seconds interval, probably stretching right along the South Coast. Satisfied at having solved this mystery, he turned the corner and ran into a police speed trap. So that was what the original man had been flashing him about!

'But I still think my original theory holds good for all other cases,' says Kington.